China Since 1911

China Since 1911

GEORGE MOSELEY

1817

Harper & Row, Publishers

New York and Evanston

CHINA SINCE 1911. Copyright © 1968 by George Moseley. Printed in the United States of America. All rights reserved. No part of this book may be used or reproduced in any manner whatsoever without written permission except in the case of brief quotations embodied in critical articles and reviews. For information address Harper & Row, Publishers, Incorporated, 49 East 33rd Street, New York, N.Y. 10016.

FIRST U.S. EDITION, 1969

LIBRARY OF CONGRESS CATALOG CARD NUMBER: 71-81873

Contents

Note on the transliteration of Chinese names

Written Chinese is monosyllabic, each character, or ideograph, representing one syllable. Most Chinese names, however, consist of two or more characters, and in everyday speech are pronounced as polysyllabic words. Various systems of Romanization have been devised, but none is completely satisfactory.

The Wade-Giles system is generally used by English and American Sinologists, but many Chinese names have become familiar in a less rigorous newspaper style of transliteration. The Wade-Giles system is used in this book for most Chinese personal names (for instance, Yüan Shih-k'ai, Mao Tse-tung); the newspaper style is used for place names (such as Tientsin, Yunnan). Wade-Giles transliteration is based on Peking pronunciation, which is but one of many variations of spoken Chinese. It is therefore not used here for proper names which have become familiar in a Romanization based on another dialect: for instance, Chiang Kai-shek, which would be Chiang Chieh-shih according to Wade-Giles. Some place names, such as Canton (for Kuang-chou), are simply the invention of Europeans.

No attempt has been made to be systematic in the transliteration of names of Chinese organizations: thus, T'ung-meng hui (Alliance society) is written according to Wade-Giles, while newspaper style has been used for Kuomintang (Nationalist party). Proper names are capitalized but not italicized, while the reverse holds for Chinese terms (for instance, *hsien*, county). The guiding principle has been to avoid making Chinese history seem stranger than it really is. For this reason, the English renderings of such well-known entities as 'Chinese Communist Party' has been employed rather than their less familiar Chinese names (in this case, Kung-ch'an tang).

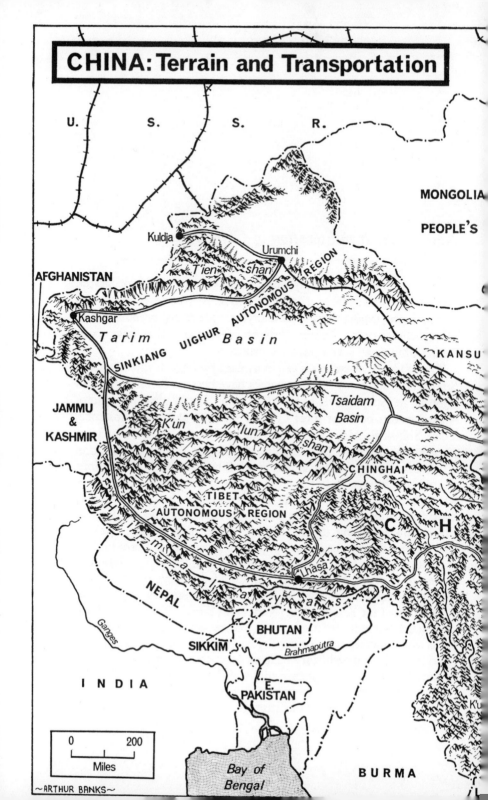

CHINA: Terrain and Transportation

U. S. S. R.

MONGOLIA

PEOPLE'S

AFGHANISTAN

Kuldja

Urumchi

Tien shan

AUTONOMOUS REGION

Kashgar

Tarim Basin

SINKIANG UIGHUR AUTONOMOUS

KANSU

JAMMU & KASHMIR

K'un lun shan

Tsaidam Basin

CHINGHAI

TIBET AUTONOMOUS REGION

C H

Lhasa

NEPAL

H i m a l a y a s

Ganges

BHUTAN

SIKKIM

Brahmaputra

INDIA

E. PAKISTAN

0   200

Miles

~ARTHUR BANKS~

Bay of Bengal

BURMA

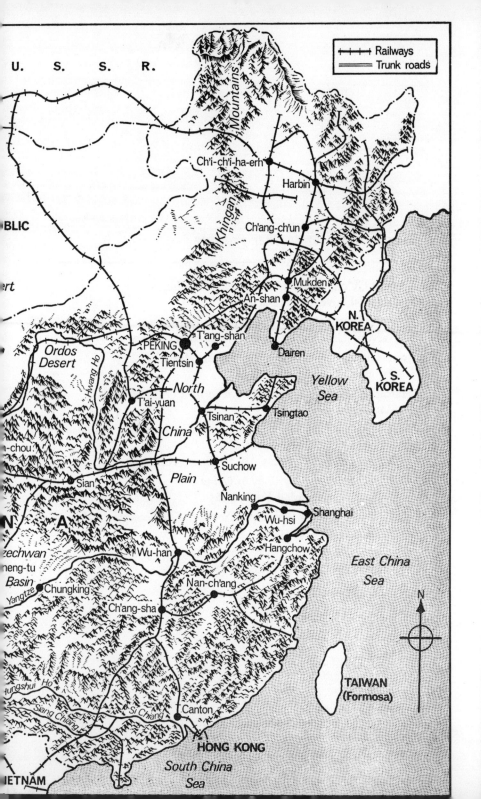

U. S. S. R.

BLIC

Khingan Mountains

Ch'i-ch'i-ha-erh

Harbin

Ch'ang-ch'un

Mukden

An-shan

N. KOREA

Ordos
Desert

Hwang Ho

PEKING

T'ang-shan

Tientsin

Dairen

Yellow
Sea

S. KOREA

North

T'ai-yuan

China

Tsinan

Tsingtao

-chou

Plain

Suchow

Sian

Nanking

N   A

Wu-hsi   Shanghai

Hangchow

zechwan

eng-tu

Wu-han

Nan-ch'ang

East China
Sea

Basin

Chungking

Yangtze

Ch'ang-sha

N

ungshui Ho

Siang Chiang

Si Chiang

Canton

TAIWAN
(Formosa)

IETNAM

HONG KONG

South China
Sea

Suggestions for further reading

Jerome Ch'en, *Mao and the Chinese Revolution*
  Oxford University Press, 1965

John K. Fairbank, *The United States and China*
  Harvard University Press, 1958 (second edition)

John Gittings, *The Role of the Chinese Army*
  Oxford University Press, 1967

Harold C. Hinton, *Communist China in World Politics*
  Macmillan, 1966

T. J. Hughes and D. E. T. Luard, *The Economic Development of
  Communist China, 1949–1960*
  Oxford University Press, 1967 (second edition)

T. R. Tregear, *A Geography of China*
  University of London Press, 1965

C. K. Yang, *Chinese Communist Society: The Family and the Village*
  M.I.T. paperback, 1965

Donald S. Zagoria, *The Sino-Soviet Conflict, 1956–1961*
  Princeton University Press, 1962

CHAPTER ONE

The Collapse of the Empire

The Ch'ing dynasty in decline

In 1644 a few thousand Manchu warriors captured Peking, bringing to an end the reign of the Ming emperors. The Ch'ing dynasty which they established endured until 1911. During this period China attained a degree of wealth and power which was not inferior to that of other great dynasties—Han, T'ang, Sung, Yuan (Mongol), Ming. By the end of the eighteenth century, however, the Ch'ing dynasty had passed its peak of greatness. Its decline, marked by the occurrence of peasant and tribal rebellions, was well advanced by the time of the Opium War (1840–42). This contest, fought over the issue of commercial access to China, resulted in a British victory and the opening of several Chinese ports to the trade of European nations. The scope of the privileges accorded Europeans and Americans in China was steadily enlarged as new demands were presented to the Ch'ing court, more wars fought, and numerous 'unequal treaties' signed.

The Western powers did not cause China's decay in the nineteenth century: they simply took advantage of it. The decay was caused by the pressure of population on the land. As had been the case with earlier dynasties, an extended period of peace brought about a rapid increase of population, only to be followed by general chaos as more and more peasants turned to banditry as their only hope of survival. Unlike most pre-modern societies, the Chinese had a sophisticated mode of land utilization which, together with a political system capable of uniting a large area, meant that the number of inhabitants tended to outrun the means of subsistence. This was especially true in the early Ch'ing period, when important advances were made in agricultural technique. During the century 1741–1841 the population of China leapt from 140 million to 410 million.

By the middle of the nineteenth century the Western powers had a vested interest in the Ch'ing dynasty, which had by then granted them so many privileges. It was in their interest that the dynasty should endure. Thus, following the successful conclusion of the Anglo–French punitive expedition to Peking in 1860, the powers lent assistance in the suppression of the Taiping rebellion (1850–64), the greatest of the peasant movements which swept China during the period of the Ch'ing dynasty's decline. The brunt of the fighting, however, was borne by newly-established Chinese armies, the traditional Manchu bannermen having proved quite powerless to stem the Taiping rebels, who were inspired by a Christian messianism. The expedient of creating Chinese armies to deal with the Taipings marked a permanent loss of authority on the part of the Ch'ing dynasty, for it remained beholden to them for the maintenance of law and order in the countryside.

Up until almost the end of the century, the Manchus attempted to strengthen China by adopting certain technical innovations of the West without abandoning the political and social precepts of Confucianism. This movement of Westernization was led by the same men who had been commissioned by the court to raise armies against the Taipings—Tseng Kuo-fan, Tso Tsung-tang, and Li Hung-chang. These were the outstanding Chinese statesmen of the nineteenth century. The attempt at Westernization, which emphasized key industries and communications which served military purposes, fell victim to the Japanese, whose more thoroughly Westernized army trounced the best that China could send against them in the Sino–Japanese War of 1894–95. The realization that Chinese institutions, as well as Chinese arms, were inadequate led to the abortive 'hundred days of reform' of 1898 in which two famous Chinese scholars, K'ang Yu-wei and Liang Ch'i-ch'ao, induced the young emperor to promulgate a series of reform edicts which were soon countermanded by the Empress Dowager, Tz'u-hsi.

Japan's success in her war against China excited the envy of the other imperialist powers. Japan had obtained the great island of Formosa. In the course of 1898, Germany, France, Russia, and Great Britain, seizing upon various pretexts, obtained leases to different parcels of territory along the coast of China. Basing themselves on these leaseholds, the powers gradually carved out spheres of influence

extending deep into the interior of China, threatening the dismember-
ment of the country. At the same time, they sponsored the 'independence' of China's vassal states: Japan seized Korea, France seized
Vietnam, and Great Britain seized Burma. Russia had earlier appropriated enormous territories in Siberia and Central Asia over which
China had once exercised suzerainty. China had also been forced to
permit the foreigners to build manufacturing plants in their concessions in Tientsin and Shanghai which were soon turning out cheap
goods with which native handicrafts could scarcely compete. Mere
commercial access no longer satisfied the powers, which now resolved
upon the physical penetration of China. The result was the Boxer
Rebellion of 1900. The Boxers, one of the many secret societies active
at the time, manifested Chinese hatred of both the Manchus and the
Europeans. The wrath of the Boxers descended with special fury
upon Chinese Christians, many of whom were murdered; they cut
down numerous telegraph lines, another symbol of Western influence.
Foreign armies intervened to suppress the Boxers, against whom
China's own armies for the most part failed to take action. The Boxer
indemnity imposed by the victorious powers, whose armies had
already looted Peking, added to China's humiliations. It was also a
crushing financial burden. China's financial situation was already
critical: to ensure payment of the US $350 million indemnity, the
powers claimed the proceeds from certain domestic taxes and made
further demands on the Maritime Customs Service, which they
already administered.

The Boxer uprising had proved a serious embarrassment to the
Empress Dowager, who had done nothing to suppress it. For a time,
she even sought to use it as a weapon against the foreigners. During
the siege of the Legation Quarter in the summer of 1900 she had
simply absented herself from the capital. When this stratagem failed,
she had tried to regain prestige among the diplomatic corps and give
her archaic regime a more modern look by lifting the ban on mar-
riages between Manchus and Chinese, by taking a positive stand
against the purely Chinese practice of footbinding, and by appointing
a board to suggest further reforms. The pressure for real reform was
tremendously increased by Japan's spectacular victory over Russia in
1904–05, which suggested to educated Chinese that Japan should be
taken as a model for China's modernization. Responding to this tide
of reformist agitation and hoping to prolong its own life, the Ch'ing
court set about reorganizing China's military and educational systems

and preparing the way for a constitution. The imperial examination system, by which China's bureaucracy had been nourished for two thousand years, was abolished in 1905. Modern schools were to be established throughout the country. In 1908 there was promulgated the 'Constitutional Principles', which looked forward to the establishment of a constitutional monarchy similar to Japan's. A Ministry of War was established in 1906 and given the task of creating a national army. Many other reforms, such as the prohibition of opium, were attempted, but by this time the court was too poor and too weak to carry out its reform movement.

The court had become more and more isolated from the country, a process which reached its culmination in the dismissal of China's leading military commander, Yüan Shih-k'ai, in January 1908. Two months earlier the Emperor Kuang-hsü and the Empress Dowager Tz'u-hsi had both passed away, leaving on the throne the two-year-old boy Pu-yi, whose father, Prince Ch'un, became regent. Pu-yi was given the reign title of Hsüan-t'ûng. Prince Ch'un was a brother of the deceased Kuang-hsü and therefore hated Yüan Shih-k'ai, whom he held responsible for the failure of the 1898 reforms which Kuang-hsü had sponsored. Yüan had at first supported the reforms but later turned against them, apparently to curry favour with the Empress Dowager, who had indicated her disapproval of the reforms. Yüan was promoted while the authors of the reforms, K'ang Yu-wei and Liang Ch'i-ch'ao, fled into exile. The Empress Dowager took over the reins of government from Kuang-hsü, who lived out the rest of his days under virtual house arrest. Yüan Shih-k'ai soon emerged as the most powerful man in China, with control of the country's only modern army. Such was Yüan's success that the Empress Dowager grew uneasy: in 1907 she attempted to diminish his influence despite the fact that Yüan had long been her strongest support. But the Manchus failed to dispose of Yüan altogether. Living in retirement but constantly in touch with his officers, Yüan occupied an ideal vantage point from which to observe the unfolding of the 1911 revolution. By choosing one side or the other, he was in a position to determine the course of events in China.

The 'Manchu-first' policy adopted by the Ch'ing court in its last years, together with its attempt to undermine provincial rights and the official class, crystallized the opinion of educated Chinese against the dynasty. The peasantry had long been seething, its discontent having found expression in the emergence of many secret societies, of which the Boxers were merely the best known. Even more dangerous was disaffection in the so-called 'New Armies' created after the Boxer uprising. Organized along Western lines and provided with modern weapons, they were susceptible to revolutionary propaganda. Another focus of discontent were the provincial assemblies, which the government initiated in the forlorn hope of increasing its authority in the provinces. Ironically, the reforms undertaken by the Manchus in the first decade of the century actually prepared the ground for the outbreak of the revolution which had long been stifled. The spark which ignited the revolutionary outburst of 1911 was struck by the T'ung-meng hui, a conspiratorial party led by Sun Yat-sen. Sun himself, however, was never in control of the revolution; he was actually in the United States when, on the evening of 9 October 1911, a bomb exploded accidentally in a basement hideout of the revolutionaries in Wuchang. Within hours this false start was followed by a revolt of government troops stationed in the city which led finally to the fall of the dynasty and the elevation of Yüan Shih-k'ai to the presidency of the Chinese Republic.

Sun Yat-sen

Sun Yat-sen did not make the Chinese Revolution of 1911, but he was its prophet. Born in a village of Kwangtung province in 1866, Sun was educated in British schools in Honolulu and Hong Kong. He became a doctor and practised in Macao. In 1894 he abandoned medicine and took up revolution. The Hsing-Chung hui, or Save China Society, which he founded in that year was dependent upon the support of the overseas Chinese. In their isolated communities in South-east Asia and elsewhere in the world, the overseas Chinese, who came mainly from the south China provinces of Kwangtung and Fukien, became quite prosperous and nationalistic. They saw that China would have to throw off Manchu rule and modernize if she were to survive and become sufficiently powerful to avoid further imperialist encroachment and, incidentally, protect the interests of the overseas Chinese. The Hsing-Chung hui attempted to seize Canton, the capital of Kwangtung province, in 1895, and in 1900 it launched a military campaign in eastern Kwangtung. These revolutionary efforts, for which Sun employed a motley assortment of secret society members and bandits, demonstrated that Kwangtung could not be easily captured by a small band of revolutionaries.

In exile, Sun sought the support of young Chinese who were

studying abroad. Like the overseas Chinese, the students tended to become nationalistic as a result of their exposure to the outside world. Many of them, ironically, had been sent overseas by the Ch'ing government as part of its policy of educational reform. The great bulk of the Chinese students who went abroad during the first decade of the twentieth century went to Japan. It was here that Sun Yat-sen joined with other revolutionaries in 1905 to form a new revolutionary organization, the T'ung-meng hui, or Alliance Society. Several existing organizations were combined to form the T'ung-meng hui. Apart from Sun's Hsing-Chung hui, the most notable of these was the Hua-hsing hui, or Revive China Society. The Hua-hsing hui was based on the key Yangtze valley province of Hunan, where it had been organized in 1903 by a Hunanese named Huang Hsing. Another Hunanese who joined forces with Sun and Huang in Tokyo in 1905 was Sung Chiao-jen, a man destined to play a prominent role in the revolutionary movement. Huang and Sung had participated in an abortive revolt in Changsha, the capital of Hunan, in the previous year. Huang, who had a flair for military tactics, actually participated in the succession of rebellions undertaken by the T'ung-meng hui. Sun Yat-sen's specialities were speech-making and fund-raising: as a result, he was generally to be found touring the communities of the overseas Chinese in America, Europe, and Asia.

The membership of the T'ung-meng hui consisted mostly of students, the majority of whom joined the organization in Tokyo. As the students returned to China, T'ung-meng hui propaganda was spread throughout the country. New adherents were gained. A special effort was made to win over junior officers in the army, many of whom attended military school in Japan. Within a few years branches had been set up in nearly all the provinces of China as well as in many cities abroad. The branches in Hong Kong and Hanoi were especially important because they provided bases for the eight revolts launched by the T'ung-meng hui in south China between 1907 and 1911. These enjoyed a measure of support from Japanese sinophiles and French officials. It was in connection with one of them, which occurred in December 1907 on the border between Kwangsi province and French Indochina, that Sun set foot on Chinese soil for the only time between 1895 and 1911; it also provided him with his only experience of actual fighting.

At the founding meeting of the T'ung-meng hui it was resolved that the new organization should devote itself to the revolutionary overthrow of the Manchu dynasty. This was the only substantive resolution adopted. Speaking at the meeting, at which he was elected chairman of the new organization, Sun told the delegates that the revolution would involve four things: 1. The overthrow of the Manchu dynasty; 2. the restoration of Han Chinese sovereignty; 3. the establishment of a republic; and 4. the equalization of land rights. The last item was neither generally understood nor widely accepted among T'ung-meng hui members. What they all did agree on was the imperative of ejecting the Manchus in order to restore China's greatness. Once the dynasty had been overthrown, a republic would somehow come into existence, but in 1905 few paused to consider how this would happen.

In the following year Sun outlined his political philosophy in an address to the T'ung-meng hui. His theories of the 'Three Principles of the People' and the 'Five-Power Constitution' were adapted from the American practice of government, which he apparently considered to be the most advanced model available. The Three Principles of the People were nationalism, democracy, and people's livelihood (or socialism). They are thought to have been inspired by Abraham Lincoln's phrase, 'of the people, by the people, for the people'. Sun's political ideas received some further elaboration in the pages of the T'ung-meng hui organ, Min-pao (People's journal). The establishment of the T'ung-meng hui marked a break between Sun and his fellow revolutionaries on the one hand, and, on the other, the constitutional reformers like K'ang Yu-wei and Liang Ch'i-ch'ao who looked forward to the establishment of a constitutional monarchy. The political philosophy of the reformers was inspired by the nineteenth-century Meiji restoration in Japan and secondarily by the monarchical systems of Germany and Great Britain.

The two last and most serious of the T'ung-meng hui's attempts at revolution prior to the successful Wuchang uprising in October 1911 took place in Canton in February 1910 and March 1911. With Sun Yat-sen off on his fifth round-the-world tour, Huang Hsing was the brains behind both. Unlike the previous revolutionary attempts of the T'ung-meng hui, these uprisings in Canton depended on the disaffected elements of the government army, especially on New Army units. The 1910 attempt was easily snuffed out, but it generated significant public support. The attempt of 1911, financed by large contributions from the overseas Chinese, was more ambitious. A series of false starts resulted in a lack of coordination among participating units, which spelled defeat for the rebels. Even so, Huang Hsing and his followers succeeded in capturing and burning the office of the Governor-General. The Canton revolution of 29 March 1911 left 72 martyrs, among whom were many student members of the T'ung-meng hui who had joined the organization in Japan. This failure brought to an end the efforts of the T'ung-meng hui to establish a revolutionary bridgehead in Kwangtung, Kwangsi, or Yunnan, the southernmost provinces of China. The Yangtze valley thereupon became the centre for a new phase of the Chinese revolutionary movement. This phase brought new leaders to the fore, while Sun Yat-sen remained merely the titular head of the movement.

10 October 1911

The revolutionary movement that led to the overthrow of an imperial system under which China had been ruled for two thousand years and to the establishment of a Chinese Republic was not the creation of a few students affiliated with the T'ung-meng hui. The active revolutionaries expressed a discontent which had become very widespread, especially in south China. The assassination of government officials, largely the work of anarchists, had become common occurrences. The Manchu governor of Anhwei province, who died at the hands of an assassin in 1907, was one of the more notable victims. Peasant risings, such as the 1910 rice riot in Hunan, were also frequent. Since recruits for the New Army came primarily from rural areas, it could no longer be relied upon to defend the dynasty and its officials, who now feared for their lives. More and more power slipped into the hands of anti-Manchu secret societies, which drew their support from the lower classes, while provincialism was the expression of upper-class opposition to Manchu rule. Political organizations like the T'ung-meng hui found it difficult to keep abreast of events. Aware that the Yangtze valley was ripe for revolution, Sung Chiao-jen had taken the lead in establishing a new T'ung-meng hui headquarters at Shanghai which was operationally independent of both Tokyo and Hong Kong.

By the time the Shanghai office of the T'ung-meng hui was opened on 31 July 1911, developments in Szechwan, far up-river, were already moving toward a climax. Szechwan is China's most populous province, and one of its richest. During the last decade of Manchu rule a capitalist revolution was taking place in Szechwan. Members of the scholar-gentry class were entering commerce and industry, and in so doing they frequently became competitors of foreign firms. A similar development was taking place in other parts of China which were comparatively open to Western influence. One enterprise which involved an unusually large number of people in Szechwan was the Chengtu–Hankow railroad, which was intended to link Szechwan with Hupei. The purchase of shares in the projected railroad had been imposed on the population as a kind of tax. The Ch'ing government, itself short of funds, was jealous of this project, which would remove from its grasp a potential source of wealth, whether as a profitable concern or simply as collateral for a foreign loan. The railroad issue was taken up by the provincial assembly of Szechwan at its first session in October 1909. Peking had encouraged the establishment of provincial assemblies in the hope that they would strengthen central control over the provinces, but they became, instead, focal points of anti-Manchu feeling. In May 1911 the Ch'ing government announced that it had secured a loan from a consortium of British, French, German, and American financial interests for the construction of the Szechwan–Hupei railroad, which would be under the exclusive management of the central government. This announcement brought Szechwan into open opposition to Peking. Fighting between the local militia and government forces occurred in September, forcing the authorities to bring in additional units from Wuhan, further down the river.

'Wuhan' is the name by which Wuchang, Hankow, and Hanyang, all in Hupei province, are collectively known. Wuchang is a walled city which, from the point of view of military tactics, dominates the other two cities. Wuhan is twentieth-century China's third most important industrial area, outranked only by Manchuria and Shanghai. But it is unrivalled as a domestic communications centre, for it commands the country's principal north–south land route as well as the middle reaches of the Yangtze River, which is the east–west artery of central China. Thus, a revolt at Wuchang could not be a purely local affair.

The New Army force in the Wuhan area was unusually large, but the security situation, from the point of view of the government, was made precarious by the susceptibility of these troops to revolutionary propaganda. Such was the plight of the dynasty that the bigger its armies, the more it was threatened. Revolutionary cells had been set up in the Hupei New Army beginning in 1908 by a local organization loosely affiliated with the T'ung-meng hui. The work of subverting the army to the revolutionary cause was carried out with such diligence that by the beginning of 1911 the leaders of the anti-Manchu cause in Wuchang began to feel confident that a revolt could succeed. Their optimism was increased by the disturbance in Szechwan, with which the Hupei gentry tended to sympathize. In mid-September an emissary was sent to Shanghai, and a message to Hong Kong, to invite Sung Chiao-jen and Huang Hsing, respectively, to come to Wuchang to take charge of the impending rebellion, but neither of them arrived in time.

On 9 October 1911 a bomb exploded accidentally in the office of the main revolutionary organization in the Wuhan area. The premises, located in the Russian concession of Hankow, were immediately raided by the police, who made some arrests and seized documents implicating many of the revolutionary leaders. 10 October was a day of terror as the authorities first beheaded those captured on the previous day and then resorted to indiscriminate arrests in order to liquidate the rebels; but in the evening there occurred an uprising of army units in Wuchang which had joined the revolutionary cause. High government officials fled Wuchang as fighting went on through the night; by morning the city was in the hands of the revolutionaries. The Manchu troops, known as bannermen, suffered heavy casualties. Being without a leader well known to the people, the conspirators proclaimed the Military Government of Hupei in the name of Li Yüan-hung, a brigade commander who had not evinced any enthusiasm for the revolutionary cause but whose Han Chinese race was, apparently, enough to satisfy the anti-Manchu revolutionaries. The proclamation of the Military Government was made on 11 October. A transitional period of military rule was in keeping with the political concepts of Sun Yat-sen, who did not believe that democratic institutions could be established immediately in China. On the 12th the garrisons of Hankow and Hanyang went over to the revolutionaries, bringing all of Wuhan under their control, and on the same day telegrams were sent to various parts of the country justifying the Hupei rebellion in the name of Han Chinese nationalism and inviting other provinces to follow suit. Hunan, which declared its independence of Peking on 22 October, was the first to do so. On 4 November Shanghai was captured from within by revolutionary forces which included workers, students, and even police. By the end of November, 15 of the 18 provinces of China proper had declared their independence, while Nanking, the key city between Wuhan and Shanghai, was captured on 3 December.

Meanwhile, the Manchu court had turned in desperation to Yüan Shih-k'ai, the only man who seemed capable of leading the imperial army against the revolutionaries. Called out of retirement, Yüan became premier of the Peking government on 1 November. By late November the best of the northern troops had been concentrated in the vicinity of Wuhan. In several days of stiff fighting they pushed the revolutionary forces, now commanded by Huang Hsing, out of Hankow and Hanyang, but they stopped short of Wuchang. While the government armies threatened Wuchang, revolutionary forces were preparing to launch an offensive against the north from several points along the Yangtze. The Western powers, which had adopted an attitude of benevolent neutrality toward the 10 October uprising, now proposed negotiations between Yüan Shih-k'ai and Huang Hsing. This Western initiative was prompted by the fear that Japan would exploit the civil war to her own advantage. Whereas the Western powers had put a freeze on loans to either side, Japan was quite prepared to extend loans to whichever side offered the most sweeping concessions. Thus, the military stalemate was perpetuated as negotiations began in Shanghai in mid-December. These led to a compromise settlement, the gist of which was that Yüan would assume responsibility for the final overthrow of the Manchus in return for leadership of the Republic. Yüan's position was strengthened by the appearance of factionalism among the revolutionaries, whose nominal leader, Sun Yat-sen, showed little personal interest in ruling China.

A provisional government was organized by the revolutionaries at Nanking. The government of the Republic would attain its final form only when, first, the dynasty had been overthrown and Yüan had assumed office and, second, when national elections had been held. On 29 December the representatives of 17 provinces elected Sun Yat-sen Provisional President of the Republic of China, and on 1 January 1912 he was inaugurated in Nanking. Sun had returned from abroad only a few days before. The provisional government was a peculiar blend of new and old. Many elderly Chinese who had served the Manchus continued in office, with T'ung-meng hui assistants assigned to many of them. Huang Hsing and Sung Chiao-jen were given cabinet posts, while Li Yüan-hung was made Vice-President. Military governors stood at the apex of the provincial administrations, which became increasingly jealous of their independence. Many of them were warlords, while the provincial assemblies, whose authority was more nominal than real, were crowded with

T'ung-meng hui members. Yüan Shih-k'ai and Sun Yat-sen could each claim the real loyalty of only a few provinces. In general, the provinces declined to remit tax receipts either to Peking or to Nanking. Desperate for funds, both governments tried to secure foreign loans: Yüan looked first to Britain, Sun to Japan. However, no large-scale foreign assistance was forthcoming until 1913. Some of the military units which the revolutionaries had assembled in the Yangtze valley had to be disbanded because there was no money to maintain them.

Sun Yat-sen's first official act as provisional President was to lead a procession bearing sacrificial tribute to the tombs of the Ming emperors at Nanking. By this symbolic act he fulfilled the greatest longing of many of those who had supported him—namely, to oust the alien Manchus. The Ming dynasty, which preceded the Ch'ing, had also overthrown an alien rule, that of the Mongols. Many of the secret societies in China had been dedicated to the restoration of the Ming dynasty. However, the new Nanking government shunned the secret societies. Although they had supported the revolutionaries, their lower-class character was no longer attractive to Sun and his group once the revolution was successful. In competition with the militarists, led by Yüan Shih-k'ai, the revolutionaries now curried favour among the new bourgeoisie, the gentry, and the interested foreign powers.

On 12 February 1912, an edict of abdication was issued in the name of the six-year-old Hsüan-t'ung emperor, later known as Henry Pu-yi. The edict specified that power was being transferred to Yüan Shih-k'ai, without making any reference to the Republic. It was Yüan, and not the revolutionaries in Nanking, who could ensure the safety of the Manchu court in Peking. On the following day Sun Yat-sen resigned and recommended that the provisional assembly elect Yüan Shih-k'ai to succeed him. This was done on 14 February, with Li Yüan-hung remaining as Vice-President. The Manchu standard of the yellow dragon was replaced in Peking by the new flag of the Republic, which had been flying over Nanking since 1 January. The new national flag consisted of five horizontal stripes in red, yellow, blue, white, and black, representing the Han Chinese and the four principal minority groups inherited from the empire—Manchus, Mongols, Moslems, and Tibetans. The five-striped flag represented a hope more than a reality, since the Mongols and the Tibetans had thrown off Chinese rule immediately after the Wuchang uprising.

The provisional assembly which endorsed Yüan's succession to Sun also drew up a provisional constitution to replace the organic law under which Sun had exercised authority since the first of the year. Whereas Sun's government had been presidential in form, Yüan was to head a cabinet form of government. The followers of Sun Yat-sen, who already had reason to be apprehensive about their political future, hoped that the cabinet would provide a check to Yüan's power. However, Yüan immediately flouted the provisional assembly by refusing to come to Nanking, which had been designated the capital of the Republic. Instead, members of the assembly had to remove themselves to Peking.

The Chinese Revolution, which began on 10 October 1911, was completed by the Manchu abdication four months later. The fall of the Ch'ing dynasty brought China's ancient system of government to an end. 10 October became the national day, and the men began cutting off the queues which had been a sign of subjection to the Manchus. The Gregorian calendar replaced the lunar calendar for official purposes, and 1912 was designated the first year of the Republic. The Republic was proclaimed on 1 January 1912, the day of Sun's inauguration as provisional president. The Nationalists, who claim to be the followers of Sun Yat-sen, continued to reckon the years in this fashion even after they abandoned the principle of the Republic and established a National government in 1928, the 17th year of the Republic. In the 38th year of the Republic, or 1949, the Nationalists quit the mainland of China to become exiles on the nearby island of Taiwan, which they regard as a province of the Republic of China. The Communists did not imitate this system of dating after the establishment of the People's government on 1 October 1949, but adopted, instead, the almost universally used Christian calendar.

The Second Revolution

During 1912 and 1913 China had its one and only experience of parliamentary democracy, or at least of a fairly close approximation to it. It proved unworkable in China, just as it has in a number of Asian countries which achieved independence after the Second World War. The Chinese experience of parliamentary democracy ended in failure because the individuals and groups who controlled the military apparatus of the country refused to contemplate relinquishing power to elected officials. Although carried out in the name of constitutionalism, the 1911 Revolution resulted in the transfer of real authority from the Ch'ing dynasty to military officers who had served the empire. For the most part, they remained Confucian in outlook, as did the gentry and the peasantry. Only the urban bourgeoisie, together with the conspirators who had actually precipitated the revolution, really understood and appreciated parliamentary democracy—an insufficient popular following to ensure its survival. The provincial and national assemblies which had been elected by limited franchise were not taken seriously by most Chinese, who felt instinctively that a surrender of power to them by the military strongmen would only bring confusion. This opinion was shared by the Western powers with interests in China.

Perhaps the most fervent supporter of parliamentary democracy in China was Sung Chiao-jen, the number-three man in the T'ung-meng hui. He was determined that the personal rule of Yüan Shih-k'ai should be restrained by an effective parliament. During the summer of 1912 Sung led in the reorganization of the T'ung-meng hui, which was combined with other political groups to form the Kuomintang, or National Party. Following a diligent campaign, the Kuomintang swept the national elections held at the end of the year. It seemed clear that the Kuomintang would dominate the cabinet, although it did not intend to challenge Yüan for the presidency. On 20 March 1913 Sung was shot at the railway station in Shanghai as he was about to depart for Peking, where the National Assembly was to convene in April. He died two days later, at the age of 30. The man behind Sung's assassination was the President of the Republic of China.

On 26 April, without consulting the National Assembly, Yüan Shih-k'ai signed an agreement for a huge loan from Britain, France, Russia, Germany, and Japan. Because the terms for repayment of the loan called for extensive foreign supervision of China's financial system, the United States had decided not to participate. The purpose of the £25 million Reorganization Loan, as it was called, was to re-finance China's existing international indebtedness and balance the books of the foreign bankers. With most of the total budget of the Peking government earmarked for the servicing of its foreign debts, Yüan well deserved his nickname, 'bailiff of the powers'. Yüan, of course, had his own purposes: he used the Reorganization Loan to crush the Kuomintang in the civil war which broke out in July.

Sun Yat-sen had not shared Sung Chiao-jen's enthusiasm for a parliamentary contest with Yüan Shih-k'ai. While Sung was building the Kuomintang, Sun had tacitly accepted Yüan's dictatorship and retired from politics. Accepting the title of Director of Railroads bestowed on him by Yüan, Sun devoted himself to a scheme for building 200,000 miles of railroads in China. But Sung's murder and the handling of the Reorganization Loan awoke Sun to the fact that he had been misled by Yüan. He now realized that Yüan would have to be opposed by force, just as Yüan realized that the Kuomintang would have to be crushed. The struggle which ensued is known as the Second Revolution.

The Second Revolution lasted from 12 July until 12 September 1913. It was precipitated by Yüan's attempt to discredit Huang Hsing, still an important Kuomintang figure in the south, and his dismissal of the pro-Kuomintang military governors of three southern provinces—Kiangsi, Kwangtung, and Anhwei. The central figure in the armed confrontation between Yüan and the Kuomintang was Li Lieh-chün, governor of Kiangsi, who declared war against Peking on 12 July. During the next few weeks most of the other southern provinces expressed support for Li, but the only serious fighting occurred in Kiangsi and around Nanking in neighbouring Kiangsu province, where Huang Hsing took the field against the northern armies. There was neither money nor popular support for the cause of the Kuomintang, and their military forces were quickly overwhelmed by Yüan. Both Huang Hsing and Sun Yat-sen fled to Japan, which had supported their cause.

Thanks to his victory in the Second Revolution, Yüan was able to extend his control over the Yangtze valley, long a Kuomintang stronghold. The Second Revolution was also a prelude to a major extension of Yüan's political power in Peking. On 10 October 1913 Yüan had himself inaugurated as President of the Republic. Since a constitution still had not been adopted, it was illegal for him to change his title from 'provisional president' to 'president', but he got around this technicality by simply forcing the National Assembly to give its approval. Once this was accomplished he dispensed with the Assembly altogether. In November he ordered the dissolution of the Kuomintang, which meant that the Assembly, in which the Kuomintang held a majority of seats, could no longer assemble a quorum. Early in 1914 he ordered the suspension not only of the National Assembly but of the provincial assemblies as well. The Republic of China won recognition from the principal foreign powers at the very time it was being emasculated by Yüan Shih-k'ai. The United States led the way in May 1913. In order to obtain British and Russian recognition, granted in the autumn of 1913, Yüan was obliged to recognize the 'autonomy' of Tibet and Outer Mongolia, which were virtual protectorates of Britain and Russia, respectively.

The Twenty-One Demands

Japan had not played a major role in Chinese affairs until the Sino–Japanese War of 1894–95, by which she annexed the rich island of Taiwan and gained a special position in Korea. As a result of her victory in the Russo–Japanese War of 1904–05, she extended her influence from Korea into south Manchuria, which the Russians had been in the process of developing. The Chinese did not take a clear-cut stand against this intrusion because they regarded Japan as the Asian country which China ought to emulate so as to become strong and powerful enough to resist Western encroachment. The pan-Asianism then rife in Japan won a positive response from nationalists like Sun Yat-sen. Sun was prepared to grant the Japanese almost any concession in China they might desire in exchange for their support for his political ambitions, but the failure of the Second Revolution placed Sun in a poor bargaining position. When the outbreak of the First World War diverted the attention of the Western powers from the Far East, the Japanese attempted to impose their will on Yüan Shih-k'ai. The Twenty-One Demands which they served on him in 1915 turned out to be an enormous diplomatic blunder which per-manently poisoned Sino–Japanese relations.

Unlike Sun, Yüan felt no sentimental attachment to Japan. He had watched the aggressive measures employed by Japan in Korea which brought on the Sino–Japanese War. And in that war he had seen the destruction of China's best army, that of Li Hung-chang. Yüan drew two lessons from the 1894–95 war: first, that the Japanese were un-scrupulous; second, that fighting foreign armies was wasteful, for a political leader could not maintain himself in China without an army. Because they knew that Yüan could not be misled by their manœuvres, the Japanese disliked him intensely. Nor was it likely that they would be able to take advantage of his unwillingness to meet them in battle, for they were restrained from making war on China by the risk of intervention on the part of the other powers. Yüan would have been a fine national leader in this moment of crisis had it not been for the fact that by 1914 he had set his heart on making himself the emperor of China. This weakness exposed him to Japanese manipulation. At the same time, however, he was able to use the aggressiveness of the Japanese to deflect his political opponents at home.

Japan's seizure of German rights in Shantung in 1914 was the prelude to her presentation of the Twenty-One Demands in the following year. At the end of the nineteenth century Germany had wrung from China certain concessions in the Shantung peninsula, especially for the construction of railroads and the opening of mines, which amounted to a sphere of influence. The German sphere in Shantung was not very different from the British sphere in the Yangtze valley, the French sphere in the provinces bordering Indochina, and the Russian sphere in Manchuria. Japan had taken over the southern half of Russia's Manchurian position in 1905. When Germany's involvement in the First World War exposed her overseas possessions to seizure by other powers, Japan sought to inherit her position in Shantung.

On 15 August 1914, a few days after the outbreak of the European war, Japan presented an ultimatum to the Kaiser's government demanding that all the German rights in Shantung be handed over to Japan. The Japanese posed as disinterested protectors of the peace, claiming that they only wished to ensure that the German sphere of interest would eventually be returned to China. Japanese military operations in Shantung were much more extensive than would have been necessary if their sole objective had been to take over German possessions in the province, which were concentrated in Kiaochow Bay, and there were many instances of Chinese civilians being mistreated by Japanese soldiers. The new Japanese sphere in Shantung was actually more extensive than the German sphere had been. In December 1914, the same month in which Yüan announced his intention to restore the monarchy, the Japanese Foreign Minister, Kato Takaaki, declared baldly that Japan had no intention of retiring from Shantung.

The Twenty-One Demands, presented in January 1915, were also the work of Foreign Minister Kato. They were arranged in five groups. The first group related to Shantung, and were intended to confirm the Japanese in the position they had attained there. The second group pertained to the Japanese sphere in south Manchuria, which included adjacent territories of Inner Mongolia. Japanese subjects were given the right to engage in any occupation and to reside at places of their own choosing in south Manchuria, which thus, in direct contradiction of the open-door principle, became a vast concession. In the demands of the third group Japan sought to ensure and enlarge her interests in the Hanyehping iron and coal complex at Wuhan, while the fourth group related to Japanese rights in Fukien province, opposite Taiwan. The fifth group contained the most sweeping of the Twenty-One Demands. They would have made China a virtual protectorate of Japan. Article one of the fifth group called upon the Chinese government to employ 'influential Japanese advisers in political, financial, and military affairs', while article three demanded that the police departments in important places in China be 'jointly administered by Japanese and Chinese'.

In presenting the Demands, the Japanese minister in Peking had warned Yüan that they must be kept strictly secret. It was in Yüan's interest that the United States government be informed, however, and Paul Reinsch, its minister to China, was perhaps the first to learn about them. As the contents of the Demands gradually became known through the press, a wave of patriotic feeling swept the country. Liang Ch'i-ch'ao's was a leading voice in protest against Japan's ambitions in China. China's indignation was also expressed in a boycott of Japanese goods as well as by a mass exodus of Chinese students from Japan. Although Yüan had the sympathy of Great Britain and France, neither country was in a position to take meaningful action, while the US contented itself with a reaffirmation of the open-door principle. As Yüan stalled, hoping for greater support both at home and abroad, the Japanese grew impatient, and on 7 May delivered an ultimatum. The Japanese threat to act if Yüan refused to yield was backed by a more subtle manœuvre. Japan intimated that further hesitation on the part of Peking might oblige Japan to support the provinces which by this time had rebelled against Yüan, whereas Peking's acceptance of the Demands would make it possible for Japan to support Yüan's imperial ambitions. The ultimatum was softened by the shifting of group five out of the Demands: they were to be 'reserved for future discussion'. On 25 May 1915 treaties were signed embodying the main points of the first four groups.

Japanese interests in China were not advanced very much by the agreements of 25 May, which, for the most part, merely restated privileges which Japan already enjoyed. Her true ambitions, as spelled out in the demands of group five, had been revealed but not realized. China had been awakened to the Japanese threat. It would no longer be possible for Chinese nationalists to be pro-Japanese. Tokyo's willingness to deal with Yüan embittered Sun Yat-sen, then in exile in Japan, and prepared him for his eventual collaboration with the Russians.

The end of Yüan Shih-k'ai

A return to a monarchist system of government was implicit in Yüan's dissolution of the National Assembly at the end of 1913. His assumption of dictatorial powers was marked by the promulgation of his Constitutional Compact on 1 May 1914. During the summer, Yüan initiated a campaign designed to demonstrate public support for the re-establishment of a monarchy, and in September he decreed that Confucius should once again be worshipped throughout the land. Chinese history was beginning to move backwards. By a bogus referendum held in the autumn of 1915, representatives of the provinces unanimously called for monarchism, and on 12 December the monarchy was proclaimed. Yüan was to ascend the throne on 1 January 1916, but a revolt in the provinces forced him to postpone and finally to abandon his plan to become emperor.

Yüan's monarchist plot had crystallized opposition to his personal rule. The opposition was led not by Sun Yat-sen and the Kuomintang but by Liang Ch'i-ch'ao and the Chinputang, or Progressive Party. The Chinputang was the party of the constitutional reformers who had advocated gradualism rather than revolution before the establishment of the Republic and who, after its establishment, generally supported Yüan Shih-k'ai. But the Chinputang, though comparatively conservative, could not accept a total abandonment of the Republic. This is an indication of the political progress China had made under the Republic, for which there had been little support at the time of its establishment. In a famous tract of 1915 Liang Ch'i-ch'ao pointed out that the answer to China's ills was to improve the administration, not to change the form of state. Such was the power of Liang's pen that Yüan had offered him a large sum of money not to publish the article, but to no avail. Liang became the focus of anti-Yüan feeling throughout the nation. Many of Yüan's own officers in the northern army opposed the monarchist scheme. Yüan could not look to the people for support, for they had no fondness for his corrupt and oppressive government. Moreover, Yüan was diplomatically isolated: even Japan had turned against his plan to restore the monarchy.

The standard of revolt was first raised in the south-western province of Yunnan. Under the leadership of Ts'ai Ao, a former governor of Yunnan and student of Liang Ch'i-ch'ao, Yunnan declared its independence in late December. Kweichow, Kwangsi, and Kwangtung followed suit early in 1916. These were the southern provinces which had eluded Yüan's grasp following the collapse of the Second Revolution three years earlier. The anti-monarchist revolt led by these four provinces is sometimes referred to as the Third Revolution. In Yunnan, Ts'ai Ao assembled a force which was called the National Protection Army. This small force, numbering only a few thousand men, marched over the mountains to the north and descended into Szechwan, where it clashed with units of Yüan's northern army. The government troops displayed little appetite for battle and failed to achieve a clear victory against the force led by Ts'ai Ao.

Unable to eliminate the insurrection, Yüan formally abandoned the monarchy in March. But this was no longer sufficient to placate Ts'ai Ao, who demanded that Yüan step down from the presidency. In April the four southern provinces which had declared their independence acted together in forming a military government with its seat in western Kwangtung. The strength of the southern cause was enormously increased in May, when Szechwan and Hunan, the key provinces of central China, declared their independence of Peking. Then, in June, Yüan died suddenly. His death, precipitated by extreme bitterness and disappointment, marked the end not only of the drama of his bid to re-establish the monarchy but of an historical epoch as well. In the same way that the names of Tseng Kuo-fan and Li Hung-chang are associated with successive periods covering the second half of the nineteenth century, so Yüan's attaches to the first decade and a half of the twentieth.

When Li Hung-chang died in December 1901, Yüan Shih-k'ai succeeded him as governor-general of the province of Chihli, in which Peking is situated, and as commander of the Peiyang, or northern army. Yüan had already shown himself to be an outstanding leader in Shantung, where he had built up a military force which was singularly successful in suppressing the Boxers. Yüan re-trained and reorganized the army he inherited from Li Hung-chang. Under his command, the Peiyang Army became an efficient organization. It was China's first truly modern army, fully equipped with the latest weapons. The Peiyang Army provided Yüan with a basis of power which made him China's strong man. Theoretically, the Peiyang Army would have been capable of engaging a foreign army, though Yüan was much too prudent to risk it in this way. Its real purpose was to overawe any conceivable domestic enemy—first of the Manchus, and later of Yüan himself. Yüan also supervised the Paoting officers' school, the leading military academy of China, and controlled the assignment of officers to various military posts. Commanders throughout the army were personally loyal to Yüan. When, after 1906, some of Yüan's units were assigned to other provinces to provide the core for the New Armies being established by the Court, the officers who led them retained their loyalty to Yüan. Nor did Yüan's dismissal in 1908 affect his standing among his subordinates. His personal eminence explains why the transition from empire to republic in 1910–11 was accomplished so smoothly and peacefully: the political revolution was contained by continuity in the military establishment. The real break with the past came with Yüan's death in 1916, for it was only then that the monopoly of power he had inherited from Li Hung-chang was broken up.

Provincialism had been made respectable by the provincial assemblies sponsored by the Ch'ing government in 1909 as well as by the earlier reform of the educational system which transferred responsibility in this field from the central government to the provincial authorities. The termination of the examination system by an imperial decree of 1905 meant the end of Confucianism. The new ladder of success was to be provided by modern schools in the provinces. The trend toward provincialism was further strengthened by the Ch'ing government's decision to establish New Armies along provincial lines, although this reform was counteracted by the authority which Yüan Shih-k'ai still exercised over the entire military establishment. Provincialism continued to grow after the 1911 Revolution, itself a victory for the provinces in their struggle against renewed dictation by Peking. Individual Chinese began to identify with the province in a way which would have been unthinkable under the empire. This new provincialism was in effect an incipient form of nationalism, and it flourished until it was rendered obsolete by the Japanese invasion of China in 1937. Yüan Shih-k'ai struggled against provincialism, just as the Manchus had, for the greater the autonomy of the provinces, the smaller was the share of provincial tax revenues forwarded to Peking. He used his authority over the military forces in the provinces to enforce his order of 1914 dissolving the provincial assemblies, but he was not able to retain the obedience of the military governors whom he put in command in the provinces. The revolt led by Ts'ai Ao in the south was essentially a revolt of provincial militarism against central authority. By the time of his death, Yüan controlled only the capital and its immediate environs.

Yüan was succeeded by the Vice-President, Li Yüan-hung, who revived the provisional constitution of 1912 as well as the National Assembly. However, President Li lacked real authority since he could not control the military leaders, who actually dominated the provinces. Within a year of Yüan's death both the presidency and the Assembly had become the hapless pawns of the generals, who now began fighting among themselves for supremacy. The years from about 1917 to about 1928 are known as the warlord era. During this period there was almost continuous fighting in one part of the country or another; untold misery was inflicted upon the people. Paradoxically, it was during these same years that China experienced a great cultural awakening and a powerful movement of the industrial proletariat. Communism made its appearance in China. At the same time, the Nationalist movement was nurtured in the south by Sun Yat-sen and finally led to national victory by Chiang Kai-shek. Chinese capitalism developed real strength. Thus, the warlord era was a time both of chaos and of creativity. During it, China reached its lowest ebb, and then rediscovered itself.

CHAPTER TWO

The Rise of the Kuomintang

The warlord era

Three incidents which occurred during the summer of 1917 dramatized the chaotic condition of the Chinese political scene: the dissolution of the National Assembly in June, the transitory restoration of the Manchus in July, and the unpopular declaration of war against Germany made by Peking in August. China then entered a period of unremitting civil war which was to last a decade. The Chinese people were already tired of war when the warlord era began, nor did they see an end to war when that era formally closed in 1928. War was endemic to China throughout the century 1850–1950. What distinguished the warlord era from other periods of China's modern history is that during the years 1917–28 there was a complete breakdown of government at the national level. In the absence of any normal political process, tests of strength among the militarists became the sole means of determining the extent of their respective domains. The strongest among them dominated Peking, the most coveted prize in the game of warlord politics. Control of the capital usually meant diplomatic recognition and access to the large tax revenues and customs receipts which were under foreign administration. Peking politics was bewildering in its variety: between the death of Yüan Shih-k'ai in 1916 and the launching of the Northern Expedition in 1926, China had six heads of state and 25 cabinets. Even without controlling Peking, a warlord might attain major status by dominating an important region of the country or by winning the support of a foreign state. A number of secondary warlords controlled individual provinces, although in some cases their authority did not extend much beyond the provincial capital. Then there were countless petty warlords, ranging down to the local bandit leader. Moreover, the camps of the great warlords were often little more than temporary confederations. With the exception of a few isolated areas, therefore, the whole of China was in a state of flux during the warlord era.

The Peiyang military party which Yüan Shih-k'ai had created remained the dominant military force in the country following his death. Tuan Ch'i-jui, first in line to succeed Yüan, adopted a pro-Japanese orientation which became notorious. His policy was to dominate the government and to reunify the country by force. Under the guise of China's participation in the First World War, Japan supplied enormous quantities of military equipment to the Peiyang militarists. In so doing, Japan won from Tuan a promise that, at the eventual peace conference ending the war in Europe, China would not press her claim to the former German rights in Shantung which had been taken over by Japan. Although 200,000 Chinese labourers went to Europe to work on military fortifications, no soldiers were dispatched. The arms obtained from Japan were used, instead, in a campaign against the southern provinces, which refused to accept the military dictatorship in the north. The fighting, which occurred in the autumn of 1917, was concentrated in the pivotal provinces of Szechwan and Hunan. Tuan was not able to overcome the resistance of the southerners, who succeeded in maintaining their independence.

The main result of the north–south war was to precipitate a split within the ranks of the Peiyang military party. The generals who had become dissatisfied with Tuan's leadership gradually coalesced into a grouping which was referred to as the Chihli clique, while Tuan and his supporters became known as the Anfu clique. The Anfu clique remained the strongest force in north China until 1920, when it was defeated in a major war with the Chihli clique. The Chihli clique was led by Wu P'ei-fu, who had adopted a pro-British orientation. In 1922 the Chihli clique defeated a military challenge from the warlord of Manchuria, Chang Tso-lin, a protégé of the Japanese. Wu P'ei-fu gradually became arrogant and began to think that he could conquer all of China. In September 1924 he initiated a second war with Chang Tso-lin, but as Wu moved his army toward Manchuria he was attacked in the rear by a nominal subordinate, Feng Yü-hsiang. Known as the 'Christian General', Feng was a client of the Soviet Union, with which he maintained overland communications from his base in north-west China. His capture of Peking in October 1924 marked the end of the Chihli clique's domination of north

China. During 1925 Chang Tso-lin attempted to extend his area of control from Manchuria southward all the way to the Yangtze valley, but he was thwarted by a general of the Chihli clique, Sun Ch'uan-fang, who established himself as the ruler of Shanghai and five surrounding provinces. Sun's power was now eclipsing that of his nominal superior, Wu P'ei-fu. In the first half of 1926, however, Chang succeeded in forcing Feng Yü-hsiang out of Peking and in the following year he established himself in the capital. Such was the situation at the time of the Northern Expedition which was to sweep China during 1926–28.

The leaders in south China were also warlords, although they appear to have been less unprincipled than were the northern warlords. Sun Yat-sen tried to work with them but was finally rejected because of his uncompromising hostility to the northern militarists. The southern warlords were political realists: they supported Sun only when it suited their own purposes. In 1917 the southerners raised the banner of protectors of the constitution, which the Peiyang militarists were trampling upon. A separatist government was established at Canton, where many members of the dissolved National Assembly had gathered. It was supported by the same six provinces which had fought Yüan Shih-k'ai in the winter of 1915–16—Kwangtung, Kwangsi, Yunnan, Kweichow, Szechwan, and Hunan. Before the end of 1917 they were again at war with the north. Negotiations between north and south were held during 1918 and 1919 but the breach between the two parts of the country could not be healed. In 1920 the Military Government at Canton fell apart and the southern provinces began fighting among themselves. The southern warlords now called for a federal state in which the autonomy of each province would be guaranteed. One province, Hunan, adopted a constitution in 1922 which was based on the federalist idea. Its main purpose, however, was to shield Hunan's own warlord from the armies of both north and south rather than to give the people of Hunan real self-government. In the end, the federalist movement proved evanescent.

The warlord era was a time of great suffering for the Chinese people, but this was not entirely the fault of the warlords themselves. Many warlords were progressive individuals. Ch'en Chiung-ming, the boss of Kwangtung province, outlawed gambling in Canton despite the opposition of local interests. Feng Yü-hsiang carried on a life-long campaign against such social abuses as opium smoking and footbinding. The modern highways built by Yen Hsi-shan in the northern province of Shansi helped establish its reputation as the 'model province', while the military rulers of Kwangsi, in the south, endowed that province with what was probably the best school system in the country. Not a few warlords showed the influence of missionary teaching regarding individual human dignity, and some of their programmes and methods anticipated those of both the Nationalists and the Communists. At the other extreme was Chang Hsün, the warlord who was behind the Manchu restoration of 1917. At that time the soldiers of his army still wore the queue, the sign of subjection to the Manchus which had long since been generally discarded. The typical warlord was neither especially forward-looking nor especially reactionary but was simply a product of his times. He was closer to the masses than the Western-oriented members of the political parties, but he stopped short of advocating social revolution. A mark of true success for a warlord was to amass a fortune and retire to the security of the treaty ports. By 1926 there were some 25 major warlords living in Tientsin alone.

An acute agrarian crisis gripped China during the warlord era. Its basic cause was rural over-population, but it was intensified by the breakdown of public order which followed the collapse of the empire. Increasing numbers of impoverished peasants turned to banditry or joined the armies of the warlords. In their struggle for survival, the warlords tried to exact more and more from the peasantry in order to maintain their armies and increase their power. The variety of taxes multiplied, while land taxes were sometimes collected years in advance. When Feng Yü-hsiang took over Honan in 1922 he discovered that taxes had already been collected for that year, so he simply collected them for the following year. Wealthier families did their best to shift the burden of increased taxation on to the poorer families, who were reduced to tenancy or worse, while land ownership became more concentrated. Much of the rural wealth which eluded the grasp of the warlords was transferred to the cities, leading to a scarcity of capital in the countryside. Cultivation of the opium poppy, which yielded a higher cash return than food crops, was encouraged by the warlords, some of whom even imposed a special tax on peasants who refused to plant opium. Crops of rice, wheat and cotton diminished, as did the total area under cultivation. Main lines of transportation and communication were disrupted as individual warlords began taxing or operating the sections which ran through their territories. Much of the rolling stock of the nation's railroads was appropriated for military purposes, while privately owned draft animals, carts, and boats were requisitioned by individual commanders. Corvée was common.

As if to ensure the ruin of the economy, the various warlords issued their own paper money, and their budgets were devoted more and more exclusively to the needs of war. As traditional mechanisms for organizing relief broke down, the toll of human lives taken by natural disasters became extraordinarily large even for China. Millions died in the great drought which afflicted north China in 1920–21. But peasant agitation emerged primarily in the south, where by 1925–27 it had attained the proportions of the Taiping era in the nineteenth century. About the only activity that prospered during the warlord era, apart from war itself, was foreign investment, which showed a steady increase throughout the period. Since the principal warlords and the Peking government were all dependent upon external support, they placed themselves at the service of foreign interests to a degree undreamt of in the time of the Ch'ing dynasty or of Yüan Shih-k'ai's presidency. They were popularly referred to as the 'claws and teeth' of the imperialists.

The May Fourth movement

The scholar commands a rare degree of respect in China. Confucianism made him the lawyer and priest, as well as the bureaucrat, of Chinese society. When, along with China's last dynasty, Confucianism crumbled, the scholar did not vanish from the scene but simply broadened his expertise by taking up the new learning of the West, especially Darwinism and political philosophy. The country continued to look to the scholar for direction. The reformers of the late nineteenth and early twentieth centuries advocated combining Chinese values with Western methods, but this no longer appeared feasible to the next generation of Chinese scholars—those who had witnessed the break-up of the political revolution of 1911 on the hard rock of cultural conservatism. They felt that Chinese society was so rotten that nothing worthwhile could be grafted on to it. They argued, therefore, that the old society should be done away with altogether so that an entirely new one could take its place. Liang Ch'i-ch'ao, spokesman for the older generation, had been so audacious as to point out that Confucius himself had been not a conservative but a reformer, and that, consequently, reform was not contrary to the real meaning of Confucianism. For Ch'en Tu-hsiu, leader of the new intelligentsia, Confucianism was an abhorrent system which had made slaves of the Chinese people. Liang said that Confucianism should be reformed; Ch'en said that it should be extirpated.

Ch'en and his group spoke for a generation which, for the first time in China, looked to the future rather than to the past. Many of them had studied abroad. In the pages of the magazine, *New Youth*, which Ch'en established in Shanghai in 1915, they spoke out in favour of individual freedom, equality of the sexes, and scientific method; the traditional ethics, which sanctioned the subservience of one person to another and which tolerated footbinding and other abuses, was condemned. An issue which became especially prominent was reform of the Chinese written language. The classical literary style was the very embodiment of antiquity. It was as far removed from spoken Chinese, or *pai-hua*, as Latin is from modern European languages. An ideographic system of extreme complexity, it took most of a lifetime to master. This meant, first, that only a few learned it and, second, that those who did had little opportunity to learn anything outside the classical tradition. The central figure of the Literary Revolution was Hu Shih, who advocated the use of *pai-hua* in place of classical Chinese. Ch'en Tu-hsiu supported him. In the space of a few years several hundred *pai-hua* magazines mushroomed from the schools and colleges of the nation. The effectiveness of *New Youth* in spreading its revolutionary ideas was enhanced by the devastating satire of Lu Hsün, China's greatest modern writer, who was still a young man when he began contributing to the magazine.

In 1917 the *New Youth* group moved to the capital, where Ch'en Tu-hsiu had been appointed Dean of the School of Letters of Peking University. Hu Shih and Lu Hsün received appointments soon afterwards. At the end of 1916, Ts'ai Yüan-p'ei, in whom existed the rare combination of traditional scholarship and radical tendencies, had been made Chancellor of Peking University. Under his liberal regime the university became the centre of the increasing intellectual ferment gripping China.

Deeply resentful of Japanese policy in China, students all over the country had been stirred by the idealism expressed by President Wilson, who promised that American participation in the First World War would usher in a new era in international relations. During the spring of 1919 they closely watched the proceedings of the Versailles conference. They were infuriated by the revelation of the secret agreements which the Anfu government had signed with Tokyo, confirming the Japanese position in Shantung. Moreover, all the major powers, except the United States, were bound to support the Japanese view on the Shantung issue. When it began to appear that the US would not stand by her principles and Wilson's 14 Points, students from the major colleges of Peking resolved to hold a public

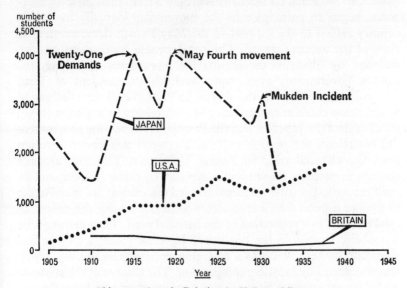

Chinese students in Britain, the U.S., and Japan

demonstration. It was scheduled for 7 May, the anniversary of Japan's 1915 ultimatum on the Twenty-One Demands, which had become 'national humiliation day'. Under the threat of government interference, however, the date for the protest rally was moved up to 4 May. On that afternoon about 3,000 students assembled in T'ien-an men square. Hoisting patriotic banners, they marched to the Legation Quarter but were denied access to representatives of any of the Western powers. Frustrated and angry, the students then burned the house of Ts'ao Ju-lin, who had negotiated the Twenty-One Demands with Japan, and beat Chang Tsung-hsiang, who had been Chinese Minister to Tokyo at the time. A third person denounced by the students was Lu Tsung-yü, Chang's predecessor as Minister to

Japan. These three men personified the pro-Japanese policy of the Anfu clique. Police, who remained passive until the very end of the demonstration, arrested 32 students.

The release of the arrested students became the new rallying cry of the movement. Classes were boycotted and appeals sent to organizations all over the country for support; at the same time, the students continued to agitate for firm government action over the Shantung issue. Girl students, traditionally segregated from their male counterparts, began to participate in the movement. Virtually the whole country rallied to the support of the May Fourth demonstrators as news of the incident spread. The pro-Japanese government was denounced by Shanghai merchants, the newspapers of Peking, the Canton government; even many warlords independent of Tuan Ch'i-jui's clique joined in the chorus. In Paris, the Chinese delegation at the peace conference was deluged with telegrams urging a strong stand against the Japanese and the Powers. However, the government did not relent, and on 9 May Ts'ai Yüan-p'ei was forced to resign from the chancellorship of Peking University. The government's attempt to suppress the student movement by threat of force, and its indifference to the students' demands, led the student union of Peking to declare a general strike; students went out among the people to awaken them to a realization of the national peril. They discovered a formidable weapon in the boycott of Japanese goods, a step enthusiastically backed by China's emerging entrepreneurial class which was threatened by Japanese competition. The alliance of the students with Chinese business interests was a combination which finally succeeded in bringing the government to its knees.

During the First World War, the movement of manufactured goods from Europe to China fell off sharply, while European demand left little American production for export to the Far East. This provided a welcome opportunity for Chinese industry which, owing to foreign control of the customs administration, had never enjoyed effective tariff protection. The number of native factories rose dramatically. In cotton textiles, the most important of China's modern industries, the number of spindles in Chinese spinning mills increased from 700,000 in 1916 to over 2,000,000 in 1922. Reflecting the increase in domestic match production, imports of Japanese matches fell in 1920 to a mere one-sixth of the 1912 level. There was also a dramatic expansion of flour milling which, outside Manchuria, was almost exclusively in Chinese hands:

Years	No. of new flour mills
1901–05	11
1906–10	17
1911–15	52
1916–20	58
1921–25	35

Foreign-owned plants shared in the boom. It was largely the Japanese who benefited, cigarette manufacture being one of the few light industries in which Western firms maintained their relative position. In the commercial, as in the political, realm the Japanese threat now overshadowed that of Great Britain, the Western power with the most diverse interests in China. Thus, there was a predisposition on the part of Chinese industrialists to support the May Fourth movement, which was specifically anti-Japanese in its nationalistic fervour. In many respects, the May Fourth movement may be seen as the cultural expression of the development of capitalism in China. Its iconoclasm was really pro-Western, for it meant to supplant China's feudal heritage with those two great hallmarks of contemporary Western civilization, science and democracy. There was nothing incongruous about the popularity of John Dewey and Bertrand Russell, who lectured in China in 1919 and 1920, respectively. This foreignness of the May Fourth movement was also its weakness, for it remained alien to the rural masses.

China's industrialists could serve their own interests by espousing the patriotic cause of the students, and they supported the boycott of Japanese merchandise which the students proclaimed. Straw hats, made in Japan, disappeared, and Chinese rickshaw-men refused Japanese customers. In June the government resorted to mass arrests of striking students, who were carrying on a vigorous word-of-mouth campaign to spread the boycott. Prompted by the students, who appealed to their sense of patriotism, merchants replied with a strike of their own. Chinese shops, factories, and banks closed in Shanghai on 5 June, and the Chinese chamber of commerce announced that the merchants' strike would continue until the students, jailed in university buildings commandeered by the government, were released. The solidarity of the protest movement was enhanced by the adherence of industrial and railroad workers, who walked off their jobs to show their sympathy for the students' patriotism.

The government found itself in a dilemma. It was under pressure from the Japanese to suppress the movement, yet every effort at repression had only made the situation worse. With the modern sector of the country virtually paralysed, the government had no choice but to give in, even though this meant jeopardizing the Japanese support which was its mainstay. The students emerged triumphantly from their detention on 6 June. The government had conceded the principal demands: the dismissal of the notoriously pro-Japanese officials, Ts'ao, Lu, and Chang, and acquiescence in the refusal of the Chinese delegation at Versailles to sign the peace treaty.

The two great scourges of China which the May Fourth movement opposed—warlordism and imperialism—could not be eliminated at a single stroke, but by mobilizing the opinion of the whole country against them it showed that they were not invincible. China took a new pride in itself. Modern Chinese nationalism was born. Even at the moment of triumph, however, the forces which had fused in the May Fourth movement were split according to their divergent analyses of the struggle ahead.

Establishment of the Chinese Communist Party (CCP)

The May Fourth movement contained a contradiction, for while it was essentially a cultural revolution inspired by the individualism and empirical method of the West, its political implications were anti-Western. The feudalism by which the Chinese were oppressed was supported by warlordism, which was in turn supported by imperialism. The effort to create a new Chinese society, therefore, would have to be anti-Western. The tendency for the May Fourth movement to flow into more and more radical channels, leading finally to Communism, was caused by this dilemma, which was inherent in the movement itself. That the Chinese revolution would ultimately require the assistance of the Soviet Union was indicated in the summer of 1919 by the hostile reaction of the powers to the May Fourth movement, which was enthusiastically applauded by the Russians. While student agitation was being suppressed in the foreign concessions, the new government in Moscow announced its determination to break with the past by renouncing all special rights acquired in China by the Czarist regime. It went on to denounce the other powers for clinging to theirs.

In their insistence on the maintenance of the *status quo* in China, the powers did everything possible to hinder the opening of channels of communication between the Chinese and the Russians. At the same time, they were aiding the counterrevolutionary forces in Siberia which were struggling against the Bolsheviks in the Russian civil war. The United States, Britain, France, and Japan participated in this venture, which began in August 1918. Japan had the largest contingent of troops in the Siberian intervention. Under the wing of the Japanese, Chinese troops of the Anfu government moved into north Manchuria and Outer Mongolia, which had been Russian spheres of influence. In Manchuria they took over the Chinese Eastern railroad, the Russian-built link between Vladivostok and the Trans-Siberian, while in Outer Mongolia they forced the authorities to cancel the country's autonomy and to ask that Chinese sovereignty be once again extended to it. Mongol autonomy had been supported by Russia. In July 1919 Tuan Ch'i-jui's War Participation Army was renamed the Frontier Defence Army. Its anti-Communist purpose was apparent to all. Since the hated Anfu government had allied itself with Japan in an anti-Communist cause, the May Fourth movement which was directed against Tuan's pro-Japanese policy tended to make the Bolsheviks appear as an ally of Chinese radicals. Even if the Russians had remained entirely passive, circumstances would have made China's youth look to Moscow.

The basis for Soviet relations with China was laid down in the Karakhan declaration of July 1919. The most remarkable feature of the China policy of the Soviet government was its stated intention of renouncing extra-territoriality. This step was formally taken in an agreement signed between the two countries five years later, but in practice the Russian nationals in China, numbering about a quarter of a million, lost their extra-territorial privileges almost immediately following the Karakhan declaration. Unlike other foreigners, the Russians were then exposed to the rigours of the Chinese penal system. The evident Soviet intention of treating with China on a basis of equality was truly revolutionary in the context of China's second-class international status. Britain, the United States, and other major powers did not follow suit until the Second World War —too late to win any goodwill from the Chinese. An exception was Germany, which, following the Versailles conference, agreed to the abrogation of consular jurisdiction over its subjects in China. The Karakhan declaration also terminated all unequal treaties existing between Russia and China and renounced further payments of the Russian share of the Boxer indemnity, a step taken by the United States in 1908.

However, the Karakhan declaration made no mention of Outer Mongolia, nor did it dispel Chinese misgivings concerning the Soviet attitude toward the Chinese Eastern railroad, although at one point the Soviet government declared its intention of restoring the line to China. Lack of understanding on these two points made it difficult for normal relations to be established between the two states. The attitude of the powers toward such a normalization was indicated by Russia's exclusion from the Washington conference of November 1921–February 1922, despite the fact that its announced purpose was to discuss Far Eastern problems of obvious interest to Moscow. The Washington conference manifested the anxiety of the powers concerning the maintenance of the *status quo* in Asia, which both the Japanese and the Russians threatened to disrupt. The conference marshalled support for the warlord government in Peking, then in the hands of Wu P'ei-fu, and had the effect of outlawing the Canton government of Sun Yat-sen. A new banking consortium, representing Britain, France, the US, and Japan, was to make loans only to the Peking government. The Anglo-Japanese alliance was terminated and Japan was obliged to withdraw her troops from both Shantung and Siberia. If Japanese ambitions were restricted elsewhere, the conference tended to endorse her position in Manchuria. The Chinese delegation received no satisfaction in response to its demand for the abrogation of the unequal treaties.

Largely because of the anti-Soviet stand of the powers, it was not until May 1924, following Great Britain's recognition of the Soviet government, that relations were finally normalized between Peking and Moscow. By that time, however, Soviet influence over the Chinese revolutionary movement had grown enormously. This influence was exerted through Comintern channels and was largely independent of formal state relations. The Comintern (the Communist, or Third, International) was established in 1919; the Chinese Communist Party in 1921. The shift in the Chinese intellectual climate which was to prove decisive occurred in 1920. It was during that year that a number of the outstanding leaders of the May Fourth movement, including Mao Tse-tung, embraced Leninism as China's salvation, thereby bringing to a climax the frantic search of China's intelligentsia for a comprehensive system of thought and guide to action which could take the place of Confucianism. Members of the Kuomintang as well as of the Chinese Communist Party were swept along in the Leninist tide of the early 1920s.

In April 1920 a Comintern representative named G. N. Voitinsky met Li Ta-chao in Peking and converted him to Leninism. Li was one of a group of Chinese intellectuals who had turned to Marxism in 1918 and 1919. Disappointment with the failure of republicanism in China and disillusionment with the West prompted by the First World War had made them receptive to Marxism by the time of the Russian Revolution of October 1917. Up until that time, Marxism had been less influential than anarchism among Chinese intellectuals. Voitinsky made them understand more fully the contribution which Lenin had made to Marxism. Lenin's theory of imperialism was of obvious applicability to China—so much so that the Chinese revolution then dawning was much more of an anti-imperialist than an anti-capitalist revolution. Li had already observed that China was oppressed by capitalism even though capitalism was not highly developed in China. This insight was given new cohesion and significance by Lenin's theory of imperialism. Lenin's notion that a revolution must be led by a tightly organized party apparatus also appealed to Li, who realized that the apathetic Chinese masses could accomplish little on their own. Intellectuals in China had a tradition of leadership in a society in which capitalism had never been highly regarded.

Li Ta-chao was the librarian at Peking University. He had joined the magazine *New Youth* in 1918, when Mao Tse-tung had worked as his assistant in the library. Under Voitinsky's influence, the group around Li was organized into a Marxist study group. During his 1920 visit to China, Voitinsky also went to Shanghai, where he met Ch'en Tu-hsiu. Ch'en had re-established himself and *New Youth* in Shanghai after having been jailed in Peking for his radical activities. A Marxist study group in Shanghai, with Ch'en as its guiding spirit, was established under Voitinsky's influence. The Shanghai group, established in May 1920, was actually the first to be set up, formation of the Peking group being delayed until September. Another such Marxist study group was established at Changsha, Hunan, under Mao Tse-tung, and others were formed at Wuhan and Canton. In November a new magazine, *Communist*, began to appear in Shanghai, where a Socialist Youth League had been established in August. In the following year Liu Shao-ch'i, a leader of the Socialist Youth League, left on a study trip to Moscow. Ch'ü Ch'iu-pai had already gone there as a newspaper correspondent. In Paris, a Young China Communist Party was established by Chou En-lai, Li Li-san, and others in February 1921. All of these persons were later to become prominent in the Chinese Communist Party.

In July 1921 representatives of the various Marxist study groups met in Shanghai for the First Congress of the Chinese Communist Party. The delegates were urban intellectuals, representing Canton, Peking, Changsha, Shanghai, Tsinan (Shantung), Tientsin, and Wuhan. These were precisely the places of maximum Western influence in China. The conferees could agree on little at their two-week meeting. It is the only congress in the Party's history which failed to issue a manifesto. Neither Li Ta-chao nor Ch'en Tu-hsiu was able to attend the First Congress, but Mao Tse-tung and Chang Kuo-t'ao were among the dozen persons who did. The policy adopted by the Party at this formative meeting was one of uncompromising hostility to all other political organizations. Both Sun Yat-sen's Canton government and the northern warlord government were condemned. A proletarian revolution on the Russian model was anticipated, and the order of the day was the organization of the industrial workers. The new Party was to join the Comintern, which was represented at the meeting, and monthly reports were to be sent to the Comintern's Far East office at Irkutsk, in Siberia. 1 July 1921 has become the official birth date of the CCP. At the end of the year, a Central Executive Committee of the CCP was organized at Shanghai, with Ch'en Tu-hsiu as secretary-general.

Despite the fact that the Russians had helped to organize the CCP, they never believed that it would actually be able to seize power in China. Instead, Moscow's chosen instrument was Sun Yat-sen's nationalist movement, consistently shunned by the Western powers. At its Second Congress, held in Moscow during the summer of 1920, the Comintern had adopted the line that bourgeois-democratic revolutions in colonial and semi-colonial countries should be supported by Communists in those countries and by the Comintern. Only after the completion of bourgeois-democratic revolutions would there be any prospect for the success of proletarian revolutions in colonial and semi-colonial countries. For Communist parties to take precipitate action in such countries, where conditions for a proletarian revolution did not exist, would be premature and futile. However, Communists in such countries could form a revolutionary vanguard within the nationalist movement and thus contribute to the anti-imperialist cause of the Comintern. These ideas were presented to the congress by Lenin in his famous 'Theses on the National and Colonial

Questions'. It is not surprising, therefore, that Kuomintang as well as CCP members took part in a Congress of the Toilers of the Far East which met in Russia in January 1922, while the Washington conference was still in session. The project for a KMT–CCP alliance was intimated at this congress, endorsed by the CCP at its Second Congress in July 1922, and accepted by Sun Yat-sen in the following year. By the end of 1923 the KMT–CCP alliance was a fact.

Reorganization of the Kuomintang (KMT)

Sun Yat-sen had twice been driven from Canton by the time he concluded his historic pact with the Soviet representative, Adolf Joffe, in 1923. In 1917–18 he headed a constitutionalist government supported by a coalition of southern warlords, but he left Canton when it became clear that he lacked real power. After a two-year sojourn at his villa in the French concession in Shanghai, Sun returned to Canton in 1921 under the protection of the Kwangtung warlord, Ch'en Chiung-ming. Although given the title of President of the Republic of China, Sun could neither strengthen his position in Kwangtung nor project it northward. In 1922 he repeated the attempt first made in 1918 to launch a Northern Expedition. Ch'en, with British support, then turned against him. On this occasion Sun had to take refuge on a Chinese gunboat before he could return to Shanghai. The escape was made possible by the loyalty of China's tiny navy, which had consistently supported the constitutionalists against the northern warlords. On board with Sun was Chiang Kai-shek, a young army officer who had become one of his most faithful adherents. His second failure in Canton prepared Sun for his policy of alignment with Russia, yet Sun's return to Canton in February 1923 was made possible by an opportunistic alliance with Yunnan and Kwangsi warlords, who drove Ch'en Chiung-ming out of the city.

The KMT–Soviet alliance was initiated on 26 January 1923, when a joint communiqué was issued by Sun and Joffe in Shanghai. On a visit to Peking in the autumn of 1922, Joffe had been enthusiastically welcomed by the intellectual community, but he had had no success in his attempt to open negotiations with the Wu P'ei-fu government. Joffe arrived in Shanghai amidst rising Chinese sentiment against imperialism and warlordism. In the communiqué, Joffe said that the Russian people stood by the Chinese people in their struggle for national unification and complete independence, while Sun observed that Communism and the Soviet system of government were not appropriate to China's needs at that time. Soviet–KMT negotiations continued during the summer of 1923. They were carried on in Japan between Joffe, who was recuperating from an illness, and Liao Chung-k'ai, one of Sun's closest associates. At the same time, Chiang Kai-shek was despatched to Russia to study the organization of the Red Army. In China, the year 1923 was marked by a series of events which further disillusioned the intelligentsia with the existing state of affairs. First came the massacre of 7 February, in which troops of Wu P'ei-fu, instigated by British officials in Hankow, attacked striking workers of the Hankow–Peking railroad in order to check the labour movement which had been gaining strength against both Chinese and foreign firms in central China. Thirty-six strikers were killed by gun-fire, while, as a lesson to other agitators, the local labour leader was publicly decapitated when he refused to call an end to the walkout. In March the student movement flared up again when Japan rejected a demand from the Peking government for the return of the Liaotung peninsula to China. The lease of the peninsula, the hub of Japan's position in Manchuria, had been forcibly extended by the treaties resulting from the Twenty-One Demands of 1915; otherwise, it would have expired in March 1923. Boycotts and demonstrations of the kind which had erupted in May 1919 re-appeared when Japan declined to discuss the matter. Then, in October, there occurred the scandalous election of Ts'ao K'un to the presidency of China. Ts'ao, the titular head of the Chihli faction and close associate of Wu P'ei-fu, openly paid 5,000 Chinese dollars for the vote of each parliamentarian. However, this did not prevent the immediate recognition of his government by the powers. Small wonder that Canton became the Mecca for nationalistically-minded youth following the establishment there of the dynamic, new Kuomintang regime.

The Kuomintang took on a steadily more radical colouring as, in accordance with Sun's understanding with Joffe, it began receiving Soviet advisers and admitting CCP members to its ranks. Michael Borodin, the chief Soviet adviser, arrived in Canton in September 1923. His assignment was to assist in the reorganization of the KMT along the lines of the Soviet Communist Party. A committee system, based on the Leninist principle of democratic centralism, was substituted for Sun's personal leadership. By January 1924, when the reorganized Kuomintang held its First National Congress, Soviet influence over the Party had become very marked. The congress laid down three broad policies: alliance with the Soviet Union, collaboration with the CCP, and organization of workers' and peasants' unions. In a stirring manifesto, the congress denounced feudalism and imperialism and announced that the KMT would energetically struggle for the realization of Sun's Three Principles of the People. During the next few months Sun delivered a series of lectures on his Three Principles, which had never been sharply defined. In these lectures he made it clear that his first principle, that of nationalism, meant anti-imperialism, and that his third principle, that of the people's livelihood, meant socialism. His second principle—democracy—was left dangling. Although Sun had gone far in the direction of ideological accommodation with his Soviet allies, he remained opposed to the concept of class struggle.

A key element in Leninist theory is the subordination of the army to the party. This was one of its great attractions for Sun, whose disappointments at the hands of the warlords had demonstrated the need for the Kuomintang to have its own army. Chiang Kai-shek also accepted this principle. After his return from the Soviet Union in December 1923 his main concern was the establishment of a military academy to train politically-minded officers. With Soviet money, arms, and advisers, the Whampoa military academy came into existence in May 1924. It was situated a few miles down-river from Canton. Chiang was made military commandant, while Liao Chung-k'ai was put in charge of political affairs. Whampoa attracted patriotic youth from all over the country, but those from Chekiang, the native province of Chiang Kai-shek, and Kwangtung were especially numerous. Political training at the academy consisted almost exclusively of the Three Principles of the People, but for many of the cadets Chiang was the personification of Sun's ideas and they developed a tenacious loyalty to him. He inculcated what became known as 'the Whampao spirit'. Chou En-lai, who was in charge of political training, could do little to check the growth of the Chiang Kai-shek mystique. Few real Communists graduated from the school, an exception being Lin Piao, the future Army Chief-of-Staff of the People's Republic of China, who was a member of the first class of cadets. The Whampoa academy under Chiang soon developed into a counterweight against Communist influence within the Kuomintang.

During its first year of existence the revolutionary Kuomintang organization in south China was threatened by a variety of enemies. In the autumn of 1924 the Kuomintang mobilized the few units of warlord troops on which it could rely to put down the Canton

Merchants' Volunteer Corps, whose mission was to protect Canton businessmen from the financial exactions of the Kuomintang and to guard against the feared Bolshevization of the city by the Kuomintang. During the first half of 1925 the warlord troops from Yunnan and Kwangsi were driven from Kwangtung and the power of Ch'en Chiung-ming in the eastern part of the province was smashed. The Yunnan and Kwangsi forces had initially supported Sun's return to Canton, but they soon showed that they were only interested in using Sun's name to cover their exploitation of the province. In expelling them from Kwangtung, the Kuomintang also consolidated its hold on Kwangsi. The Whampoa cadets contributed to the success of these campaigns, but an even more important role was played by the workers and peasants whom the Communist members of the KMT had been organizing in Kwangtung. On 1 July 1925 the Nationalist government was formally established at Canton, but by this time Sun Yat-sen had died, exposing his movement to internal dissension.

In October 1924 the Chihli clique which had dominated Peking since 1920 was overturned by a coalition of warlords led by Feng Yü-hsiang. Sun had long considered the Chihli clique the principal obstacle to the realization of his dream of reuniting and rebuilding China. His enemy in Kwangtung, Ch'en Chiung-ming, was affiliated with the Chihli clique, which had the support of Great Britain in both north and south China. Feng and his associates, on the other hand, realized that the Kuomintang had become a potent political force throughout the country. To placate public opinion and make their own position more secure, they invited Sun Yat-sen to Peking for consultations on the form that the new government should take. Sun journeyed north in November and became seriously ill in the following month. Britain, France, the United States, and most of the other powers had firmly opposed Sun ever since the consummation of his alliance with the Soviet Union, if not before, and they helped to prevent a reconciliation between him and the northern warlords. Sun died in Peking on 12 March 1925, leaving behind him political instability in both north and south China.

Liao Chung-k'ai, perhaps the most outspoken radical within the Kuomintang, was assassinated in August 1925. The party's anti-Communist right wing was discredited because of its involvement in the murder. Withdrawing from Canton, it assembled in Peking to denounce the pro-Soviet orientation of the Kuomintang and later established a separate organization in Shanghai. Meeting in January 1926, the Second National Congress of the Kuomintang overwhelmingly endorsed the leftist policies adopted at the First Congress two years earlier. Liao's assassination was the beginning of the end for KMT–CCP cooperation, which had depended so much on Sun Yat-sen.

In March 1926, Chiang Kai-shek staged a virtual coup d'état which enabled him to free himself from the control of the leftist-dominated political apparatus of the KMT and from the restraining influence of the Soviet advisers at Whampoa. Chiang's new position of authority was confirmed by a KMT Central Executive Committee meeting of 15 May, which clamped new controls on the Communists within the Kuomintang. This was a defeat for the leftist Wang Ching-wei, who thereupon resigned from the chairmanship of the Central Executive Committee and went abroad. One of the leading principles of Sun Yat-sen's entire programme, that of the army's subservience to the party, was being turned upside down, and Chiang Kai-shek had begun his spectacular rise to power. Neither Chiang nor Moscow was ready for a complete break, however, and their relations were temporarily mended. As a condition for further collaboration with the Russians, Chiang made them agree to an early launching of the Northern Expedition. Since Sun's death, Communist activity among the workers and peasants had been increasing rapidly enough to seriously alarm the more conservative elements of the Kuomintang, with which Chiang was gradually becoming identified. He feared that if the Northern Expedition were too long delayed, the Communists would be able to build an impregnable position among China's rural and urban masses.

The Northern Expedition

The industrial revolution which was sweeping in upon China by the time of the First World War created an industrial proletariat as well as a capitalist class. Chinese labour unions made their debut in Canton, which was favoured by a relatively liberal regime after 1917. They soon spread to Shanghai, Wuhan, and other cities. The Nationalist revolution led by the Kuomintang followed this same geographical pattern. Both the consolidation of the Kuomintang's hold on Kwangtung in 1924–25 and the Northern Expedition which extended its power to the Yangtze in 1926–27 were greatly aided by the newly organized workers. Peasant leagues were being organized at the same time, and their political significance rivalled that of the labour unions. There was an important difference between the two: the industrial proletariat struggled against both foreign and domestic capitalists, while the poor peasants had only one enemy, the Chinese landlord-gentry class.

The first true labour unions in China were organized in 1920, the same year that saw the creation of the first Chinese Communist cells. The mechanics' union in Shanghai and the seamen's union in Hong Kong were among the first to appear. On 13 January 1922 the Hong Kong seamen began a strike. It had its headquarters in Canton and undoubtedly had a profound influence on Sun Yat-sen. The strike, in which 60,000 workers took part, ended victoriously in March. Later in the same year a strike led by Liu Shao-ch'i and Li Li-san at the Hanyehping complex in Hupei was also successful, as were many others in various parts of the country. On May Day 1924 nearly 200,000 workers marched in Canton, and in the following year a strike against a Japanese textile factory in Shanghai led to the famous May Thirtieth movement. On 15 May a Chinese worker was shot and killed by a Japanese foreman who was trying to prevent the strikers from breaking into the factory and wrecking it. The union, supported by students and the CCP, responded with a big demonstration on 30 May. A dozen marchers were killed and 50 wounded when they were fired upon by a detachment of International Settlement police under a British sergeant. This incident led to strikes, boycotts, and demonstrations in Shanghai and many other cities. A demonstration in Canton was fired upon by French and British machine-gunners, resulting in the death of 52 workers and students and the wounding of more than a hundred. A general strike followed in Hong Kong which paralysed the colony for more than a year. Like the May Fourth movement of 1919, the May Thirtieth movement of 1925 was in large part a protest against the privileged position of the foreign powers in China. The May Thirtieth movement did not stop there, however, for it had given birth to a Communist-dominated Shanghai General Federation of Labour which helped to organize a record number of strikes—over 500—in 1926 and to boost union membership to an all-time high by the spring of 1927. The new-found solidarity of the Chinese proletariat produced a strong anti-Communist reaction among the big bourgeoisie and the warlords, who were, of course, warmly applauded by foreign business interests. Before Chiang Kai-shek entered Shanghai in March 1927 he would have to decide whether he was going to support the revolution or the counter-revolution. The upsurge of the peasant movement which took place while the Northern Expedition was in progress helped him to decide in favour of the latter.

The peasant associations represented a new form of protest on the part of the long-suffering Chinese peasant. Secret societies and banditry could not cope with the problems which now confronted him. These sprang from the commercialization of the rural economy which was an indirect effect of the impact of Western enterprise upon China. The formation of peasant associations began in Kwangtung in 1921 under the leadership of P'eng Pai, the idealistic scion of a landlord family. Becoming a Communist, P'eng agitated for rent reduction and finally for the abolition of rents. By 1923 the peasant association which he led in the district of Haifeng was being imitated elsewhere in the province: within two years, 200,000 peasants in 22 counties belonged to peasant associations. Haifeng was the home of the warlord and sometime revolutionary Ch'en Chiung-ming, and the success of the peasant movement there frightened him away from the masses. It was supported by the Kuomintang, however. During 1925 the KMT sponsored a school for peasant agitators in Canton which was headed by Mao Tse-tung. Mao had been working with peasants in Hunan, but had been chased out of the province by the authorities. By the time the Northern Expedition was launched in June 1926, there was a great potential for the peasant movement in the provinces lying between Kwangtung and the Yangtze, but its growth had been checked by the warlords. The peasant movement and the Northern Expedition were mutually reinforcing: if the peasant movement burst into full vigour only with the arrival of the southern armies, it also facilitated the advance of the Northern Expedition. By the end of 1926 the peasant associations in south China are estimated to have had a total membership of ten million, and much of the countryside was under their control.

The Northern Expedition advanced in two columns, reflecting the de facto split in the Nationalist movement. The left, or Wang Ching-wei, faction advanced into Hunan, with Wuhan as its objective, while the Whampoa faction under Chiang Kai-shek took the more easterly route through Kiangsi. The forces in the left column gave full rein to the mass movement, completely undermining the warlord armies opposing them. Hankow was taken in October 1926 and the Nationalist government was transferred there from Canton in December.

Hankow soon became the gathering place for radicals from all over China. The agrarian revolt unleashed by the Northern Expedition was particularly violent in Hunan, where many landlords lost their lives. Chiang Kai-shek's column proceeded more leisurely. Most of the Whampoa officers came from southern landlord families, so they were understandably reluctant to espouse the peasant movement. Chiang finally succeeded in occupying Shanghai and Nanking in March 1927, Shanghai having already been liberated from within by a proletarian rising led by Communists.

Shanghai had long been Chiang's prime objective. He had close personal contacts within the city, which was the economic centre of China. It could provide him with the resources he needed to sustain a national government, thus making him independent of the Russians. In return for the financial support of the Shanghai capitalists, Chiang could suppress the unions which had attained such a large measure of control over the life of the city; he could also restore order to the lower Yangtze provinces which had intimate commercial relations with Shanghai. Similarly, Chiang could satisfy the demand of the foreign powers for a military strong man capable of maintaining law and order. In January 1927 the mass movement in Hankow and Kiukiang had forced the British to evacuate their concessions in these Yangtze valley cities. The anxiety of the powers about the possible future course of the Nationalist revolution was indicated by their deployment of an unprecedented number of warships along the Yangtze and the landing of marines at Shanghai and several other places.

The turning point in the fortunes of the Communists, heretofore in the ascendant, came in March 1927 at Nanking. On the 24th, Hunanese troops under Chiang's overall command systematically looted foreign houses and killed a number of foreigners. Up until that time the behaviour of the Nationalist armies had been exemplary. The incident, apparently, was an attempt by Communists to forestall a rapprochement between Chiang and the powers, but he turned it to advantage, disciplining the offending troops and executing their leaders. The powers showed their gratitude by making available to him funds from the maritime customs receipts collected at Shanghai. Early in April, while Chiang prepared for his next move, the Russian embassy in Peking was raided by Chang Tso-lin's troops. Documents were seized purportedly implicating the Russians in revolutionary activities in China, and a number of Chinese discovered in the embassy were seized. Among those arrested was Li Ta-chao: he was summarily executed along with the others.

The Bolshevik scare was at its height and Chiang was anxious to dispel all doubts about his own inclinations. On 12 April 1927 Chiang Kai-shek unleashed a 'white terror' in Shanghai. Troops and underworld toughs attacked the armed workers who were in control of the city, killing hundreds; thousands were killed in the repression which followed. Chiang's campaign against the Communist-dominated unions was extended to the area under his control, notably the provinces of Kiangsu and Chekiang which envelop Shanghai. A reaction had also set in at Canton and other coastal cities. Hamstrung by Moscow's fondness for the CCP–KMT alliance, the Communists failed to react effectively. Ch'en Tu-hsiu, the Party's secretary-general, was later to be accused of 'capitulationism' for not having responded more vigorously, but in fact he was only pursuing a course laid down in Moscow. To have done otherwise would have laid him open to charges of Trotskyism, for at that time the struggle between Stalin and Trotsky for leadership of the Soviet Party was at its height, and policy toward the revolution in China had become an issue in that struggle. Trotsky had long argued that the CCP should not allow itself to be subject to the untrustworthy Kuomintang but should independently organize workers' and peasants' soviets. When the order for a more radical policy was finally issued from Moscow in the summer of 1927, the mass movement which had raged in south China was already flickering out.

Chiang Kai-shek followed up his suppression of the Communist-led unions in Shanghai by setting up his own Nationalist government at Nanking on 18 April. The Nationalist government at Hankow responded to this repudiation by formally expelling Chiang from the Kuomintang and depriving him of all authority. Feng Yü-hsiang, the warlord of north-west China, now held the balance of power, since neither the Hankow nor the Nanking factions had sufficient strength to drive on to Peking and thus complete the Northern Expedition. Feng had announced his adherence to the Nationalist cause in August 1926, and he had aided the Northern Expedition by engaging the rear of the Peking government forces. Late in June, Feng decided to throw in his lot with Chiang Kai-shek, but he allowed Borodin, the Soviet adviser in Hankow, and leading members of the leftist regime to withdraw through his territory to the Soviet Union. The Hankow regime thereupon purged itself of Communists in order to effect a rapprochement with Nanking, which was accomplished in September. One by one the military leaders in different parts of the country followed Feng's lead and declared themselves in favour of Nanking. The persecution of Communists, labour organizers, peasant leaders, and leftists in general became nationwide and lasted nearly a year. In south China the ferocity of the counterrevolution was terrible. In Hunan and Hupei schools were closed for six months and a house to house search for radicals was made. Girls with bobbed hair were a special target of the soldiers. Probably a quarter of a million persons lost their lives in what Kuomintang official histories describe as a 'purification movement'. In January 1928 Chiang emerged as the political and military leader of a newly reorganized Nationalist government at Nanking. Japanese military intervention in Shantung prevented him from reaching Peking, but it was captured in June by the Shansi warlord Yen Hsi-shan, who had previously declared his allegiance to the Nationalist cause. On 10 October 1928 the Nationalist government was formally established at Nanking ('Southern Capital'), and Peking ('Northern Capital') was redesignated Peiping ('Northern Peace').

CHAPTER THREE

Chiang Kai-shek between the Communists and the Japanese

Chinese society at the crossroads

China between the two world wars was not one country but three: rural China, Manchuria, and the treaty ports. A thin border of Western influence tacked on to the body of old China, the treaty ports and foreign concessions contained but a minuscule proportion of China's population and area. Nevertheless, the concentration of economic, political, and military power which the concessions represented was such as to give them a very great influence over China's affairs. A sub-culture of native industry grew up in the treaty ports as Chinese entrepreneurs and tradesmen took advantage of the stable government and sound banking facilities they offered. Shanghai was the symbol of Western enterprise in China and the financial hub of the Far East. It accounted for half of the foreign trade and modern industry of China and it employed half of the country's industrial labour force; its population of four million was more than twice that of any other city in China. Among the lesser treaty ports, Tientsin and Canton were the most important commercially, while Hankow was the nearest industrial rival of Shanghai. Two-thirds or more of the modern sector of the economy which was based on the treaty ports was owned by foreigners.

Commercial enterprise was not esteemed in traditional Chinese society. That is why it had to take root under foreign protection and then, from the concession areas, begin the slow penetration of the Chinese countryside. Chinese capitalism, as well as foreign capitalism, was centred in the treaty ports. Rural China, tied to a pre-modern level of technology, was a largely self-sufficient entity. No essential commodities were required from the outside, which was why Western merchants had resorted to the smuggling of opium into China in the eighteenth and nineteenth centuries. Only a few native products, moreover, achieved a regional or national distribution pattern. These were products such as iron, salt, porcelain, and tea, which depended on localized raw material supplies, but had a wide market. Most of the daily requirements of China's peasant families—and most of China's 400 million people depended on agriculture—were grown in the few little patches of land each family possessed, or were fashioned in the home from local materials. The books and writing materials required by the intelligentsia, or the wedding gifts for which an ordinary family might save for many years, could be found in the nearby town. The wine shops, frequented by the local elite, were also to be found there. There was an intermediate range of goods—things not readily produced in the home yet not luxury items—turned out by a ubiquitous handicraft industry. Locally produced yarn, cloth, and clothing were the most important of these handicraft goods. There was a general dependence of the rural population upon handicrafts: they provided regular and essential sources of income for approximately half of all peasant families. Not to engage in the production and sale of handicraft goods was a luxury that could be afforded only by the relatively few families with enough land to provide an adequate income from agriculture alone.

The traditional economy of the countryside was adversely affected by the modern economy of the treaty ports. The effects were not constant or uniform, and instances may be found in which particular rural areas enjoyed greater prosperity as a result of the revolution which was transforming urban industry, commerce, and finance. In the main, however, the negative effects outweighed the positive effects. In terms of values, wealth took the place of such old-fashioned Confucian ideals as virtue, thereby removing moral limitations on the abuse of economic power. And the peasant was typically in debt. The new mobility of capital enabled militarists to buy up land as well as to finance business ventures. Many became great landlords, their holdings far exceeding what could normally be acquired by a gentry family. Rents went up while land values depreciated; tenancy increased while security of tenure diminished. Absentee landlordism became widespread and rent collectors became more and more merciless. These consequences were most severe in communities situated near the coast or main routes of communication—more in the east than the west, more in the south than the north. The condition of the Chinese countryside was already critical, with a considerable part of the population living below subsistence level. Together with the effects of wars and natural disasters, the Western impact led to the disintegration of rural society. The gentry suffered along with the peasantry. Because of the poor communications and staggering over-population of the countryside, the mobility of labour was virtually nil. In general, the ruined farmer could not hope to find a job in a factory, as his counterpart frequently did during the industrial revolution in the West. Nor could the landlord readily enter into a business venture, for Chinese participation in the modern sector of the economy tended to be limited to small cliques which gained dominant positions in different fields—for instance, Chinese banking in Shanghai was dominated by men from Chekiang. The plight of the countryside was made worse by the relative decline in handicraft production. Machine-made goods could be transported to the interior with relative ease, there to compete with the village-made item.

Manchuria stood apart from both the rural areas and the treaty ports of China south of the Great Wall. Chinese colonization begin-ning late in the nineteenth century and Japanese industrialization beginning only a little later soon made Manchuria the most prosperous area of China. Unlike the older parts of the country, Manchuria had a favourable ratio of resources to population. Farms here were larger, making possible a higher yield per family. The growing of soya beans and other industrial crops was made profitable thanks to an efficient transportation system. Railroad mileage in Manchuria equalled that of all the rest of China. Manchuria's foreign trade was increasing much faster than that of China proper between 1913 and 1928, and the difference was particularly noticeable on the export side. Labour was relatively scarce, so that the industrial worker was in a more favourable position than his counterpart in China. The lack of labour unions was compensated for by the fact that the Manchurian worker was not subject to the 'rural drag' which under-employment in the countryside exerted upon the worker in China proper. The influence of Japanese imperialism was much more diffuse in Manchuria than was the influence of Western imperialism on the coast of China, and it was the Japanese presence, more than anything else, which accounted for Manchuria's progress. The Japanese provided an administrative superstructure which the Chinese themselves ap-peared incapable of erecting. Manchuria enjoyed a degree of political stability and a quantity of investment capital which was not generally available elsewhere in China.

These three regions of the country increasingly came into conflict with one another. They represented different forces acting upon China, the conflict among which would decide the direction the Chinese revolution would ultimately take. Would capitalism, accompanied by bourgeois democracy, spread into the interior from the coast and establish itself throughout China? Or would the country become a protectorate of Japan, succumbing to an imperialism which had already rooted itself in Manchuria? Or would an agrarian-based system emerge in which the peasants, led by the Communist Party, would claim a preponderant political voice?

Character of the Nationalist government

The rupture effected in 1927-28 between Chiang Kai-shek and the mass movement, which he viewed as a haven for Communists, produced a political crisis within the Kuomintang. Many rank-and-file members of the Kuomintang, and not the Communists alone, had been committed to the revolutionary ideal espoused by Sun Yat-sen in 1924. Chiang's counterrevolution presented them with the choice of accepting his personal rule or giving up Party membership and all the advantages that went with it. In 1929, half of the KMT's civilian membership of 270,000 were under 30 years of age. Since at that time there were only about half a million college and middle-school students in all of China, most of whom were over 20, it can be seen that a large proportion of the country's politically-minded youth was affected by the crisis within the KMT. During 1928 the Shansi men in the entourage of warlord Yen Hsi-shan, who ruled Hopei (the former Chihli) province in the name of the Kuomintang, were installed in positions of authority in Peking and Tientsin. The local KMT leadership, which in the north had been concentrated in the universities, was not given due recognition by Nanking, and Yen was permitted to suppress the labour unions which were just beginning to develop in Peking. In 1929 the KMT outlawed the National Students' Association, a product of the May Fourth movement. Henceforth, the only student demonstrations permitted were those which were both anti-imperialist and under party supervision. In the south, the KMT contented itself with a continuing campaign of 'bandit suppression' by which it sought to root out the peasant movement and liquidate its leaders, many of whom were idealistic youths whether Communist or not. In 1929 P'eng Pai, the peasant leader from Kwangtung, was executed by the Kuomintang in Shanghai.

The Kuomintang which made up the core of the Nationalist government established in 1928 was a party without a living ideology. It was a party subject to the personal rule of Chiang Kai-shek, who exercised his control through the party's military faction. There were actually more military than civilian members in the Kuomintang by the end of 1929, and the military members' loyalty to Chiang Kai-shek was absolute. Although he held the position of President of the National Government and Chairman of the KMT Central Executive Committee, as well as Commander-in-Chief of the Nationalist armies, Chiang chose to reside on the grounds of the Central Military Academy, the name assumed by the former Whampoa academy when it moved from Canton to Nanking following the Northern Expedition. Just as the army dominated the party, the party dominated the government. In theory, the National government conformed to the principle of 'political tutelage' which Sun Yat-sen had outlined in his 1924 work, *Fundamentals of National Reconstruction*, regarded by the Kuomintang as a sort of sacred text, like the *Three Principles of the People*. In Sun's view, a period of 'political tutelage' was an essential link between military unification and popular democracy. During this period the people were supposed to learn how to practice democracy at the *hsien*, or county, level. In practice, however, the people were permitted no democratic experimentation, and the area under Nanking's jurisdiction was ruled by means of a system of collective responsibility known as *pao-chia*, a relic of China's imperial past. The era of political tutelage was not formally closed until the promulgation of the Constitution of the Republic of China in December 1946, just as the country was drifting into full-scale civil war. Apart from Shanghai, however, the government at first had firm control (as measured by its ability to collect taxes) over only three provinces—Kiangsu, Chekiang, and Anhwei. This region, which encircles and protects Shanghai, was subject to the direct military domination of Chiang Kai-shek. Most of the rest of the country was ruled by rival militarists.

Chiang's alliance with the Shanghai business world, representing international finance as well as Chinese capitalism, gave his regime a dualistic character. The alliance was marked by his conversion to Christianity and his marriage to Soong Mei-ling, a sister of Soong Ch'ing-ling, Sun Yat-sen's widow. The two girls seem to have had great influence on their husbands, but in opposite directions. Soong Ch'ing-ling was already a radical when she decided to marry Sun in 1914, during his exile in Tokyo, while Mei-ling was firmly rooted in the hybrid society of Shanghai when she married Chiang on 1 December 1927. Both girls attended college in the United States, as did their brother, T. V. Soong, who was a Harvard graduate and the kingpin of American influence in China. T. V. Soong was known as the financial wizard of the Nationalist government and served as its finance minister from 1928 to 1933. He was succeeded by American-educated H. H. Kung, who was married to T. V. Soong's third sister, Ai-ling. Small wonder that the Nationalist government was sometimes referred to as the 'Soong dynasty'. The international, and especially American, flavour of the Kuomintang regime was not due solely to the Soongs, however. In 1931 25 per cent of the members of the large KMT Central Executive Committee had attended American universities. In 1934 nearly two-thirds of the ministers and vice-ministers in the government were foreign-educated, and American training was by far the most prestigious. This group within the Kuomintang was comparatively liberal in outlook and was known as the Political Science clique. Its influence declined after 1935. In contrast, most of the major personalities in the Whampoa clique, including Chiang himself, had attended military school in Japan but were not familiar with the West. In common with many Chinese war-lords, they admired the militaristic leadership of Germany, Italy, and Japan.

The principal warlords had been given titles in the National government in the autumn of 1928, but they maintained their military and territorial positions. Chiang was determined to overcome this obstacle to national unity. The major armies were those of Chiang himself, Feng Yü-hsiang, Yen Hsi-shan, Li Tsung-jen, and Chang Hsüeh-liang. Each of these five armies had approximately 200,000 men. Together, they comprised about half the total of some 2,000,000 men for all the regularly constituted armies in China. Maintenance of these military forces was an enormous burden for the country. The Nationalist army consumed half the revenues of the Nanking government, which had the maritime customs to draw upon. The others had to live off the land. Chiang hoped to reduce the number of soldiers from 2,000,000 to 800,000. To this end, a 'disbandment conference' met at Nanking in January 1929, but when it became clear that Chiang was not prepared to share real power in exchange for the troop reductions he hoped the others would make, the conference bogged down. The problem was finally resolved by war. With the help of German experts, Chiang had been patiently strengthening his army. In the spring of 1929 he defeated the Kwangsi troops of Li Tsung-jen and drove them from Hupei and Hunan, which he was then able to tax himself. In the following year he faced a more formidable threat in the form of a combination of Feng Yü-hsiang and Yen Hsi-shan. To deal with it Chiang won over some of Feng's and Yen's commanders with 'silver bullets'—that is, he bribed them—and called on the assistance of Chang Hsüeh-liang. The latter had rallied to the Nationalist camp in 1928, a year after his father, Manchurian warlord Chang Tso-lin, had been murdered by the Japanese. The intervention of Chang Hsüeh-liang's army in north China spelled defeat for Feng and Yen, but it exposed Manchuria to Japanese aggression. In the Mukden Incident of September 1931 Japan seized control of Manchuria (in Chinese called simply *tung-pei*, or 'the north-east'). Chang Hsüeh-liang was barred from returning, and his army remained the dominant military force in north China until the outbreak of the Sino–Japanese War in 1937. The Nationalists never exercised direct control over north China, where, as southerners, they were never accepted by the people.

One of the notable successes of the Nationalist government was in putting the nation's finances on a sound basis, although this reform proved to be only temporary. In the process of recognizing the new government at Nanking the powers agreed to the principle of full tariff autonomy, but would not agree to two other demands which, like the first, derived from the 'unequal treaties' of the nineteenth century: namely, the relinquishment of extra-territoriality and the rendition of concessions and settlements. All three had been put forward by China at Versailles in 1919 and at Washington in 1921. Tariff autonomy enabled the Nationalist government to increase its revenues and also to give greater protection to Chinese industry. Nanking was extremely scrupulous about meeting its foreign debt commitments. Even in 1931, when the country was attacked by Japan and when a great flood of the Yangtze River destroyed 12 million homes, the government made its payments on schedule. Nanking's financial position was further strengthened by an effective currency reform carried out in 1935.

Military appropriations and the cost of servicing the country's outstanding debts gobbled up most of the government's revenues.

Kuomintang ideology did not call for a significant programme of social welfare. The existence of social problems was not denied, but they were regarded fatalistically. Present misery was glossed over by discussions of long-term solutions. The KMT's rural reconstruction movement, designed to win over the peasants in Communist-influenced areas, was a fiasco. A considerable programme of road-building, financed by foreign loans, was reasonably successful, but foreign trade stagnated. In the hope of dispelling some of the apathy which had settled over Nanking, a New Life Movement was officially launched in 1934 which sought to inculcate a sort of neo-Confucian puritanism. Most of the energy of the Nationalist movement was dissipated in anti-Communist campaigns. When Nanking belatedly decided to make a stand against Japanese aggression, the opportunity which the Nationalists once had of rebuilding the nation and earning popular support had already been lost.

The Chinese Soviet Republic

Thanks to the CCP's alliance with the Kuomintang, Chinese Communist strength gained rapidly during the years 1924–27. The CCP could claim no more than 1,000 members at the time of its Fourth Congress, held at Canton early in 1925. When the Fifth Congress convened at Hankow less than two years later, CCP membership had jumped to over 50,000. A large part of this increase occurred as a result of the growth of Communist-led labour unions during the May Thirtieth movement which began in 1925. Union membership reached three million in 1927. The development of peasant associations was even more spectacular, though it was more spontaneous and less dependent on Communist leadership than was the labour movement. In suppressing the Communists in 1927 Chiang Kai-shek acted on behalf of a frightened gentry and bourgeoisie. During the counter-revolution the labour unions and peasant associations were wiped out. The wages of industrial workers were actually reduced, while the oppression of the peasants became less restrained than ever. Membership in the Communist Youth Corps as well as in the Communist Party fell sharply. In full retreat, the CCP attempted a series of desperate uprisings and then withdrew into the mountains, only to be driven out of south China altogether in 1935. In the Long March the CCP shifted its area of operations from south to north China, which was shortly overrun by the Japanese. The Japanese invasion, which undermined the traditional power structure in the north China countryside, presented the Communists with a fresh opportunity. The party which led the peasant rebellion in north China and finally captured national power was not the same CCP which had been driven from the south. A new leadership had emerged. Ch'en Tu-hsiu and the other Westernized intellectuals who had made their headquarters in Shanghai had, with a few exceptions, been replaced by a new group, led by Mao Tse-tung, which was close to the harsh realities of rural life in China.

The CCP Central Committee in Shanghai was not impressed by Mao's now famous 'Report on the Peasant Movement in Hunan' of February 1927, in which he said that what Sun Yat-sen had failed to achieve in 40 years of revolutionary effort had been accomplished by the Hunanese peasants in a few months. Mao predicted that the peasantry rather than the industrial proletariat would provide the main strength for the revolution in China. Responding to criticisms of peasant 'excesses', he remarked:

Revolution is not a dinner party, nor a literary composition, nor painting, nor embroidering. It cannot be done so delicately, so leisurely, so gentlemanly, and so 'gently, kindly, politely, plainly, and modestly' [quoting Confucius]. Revolution is insurrection, the violent action of one class overthrowing the power of another. An agrarian revolution is a revolution by the peasantry to overthrow the power of the feudal landlord class. If the peasants do not apply great force, the power of the landlords, consolidated over thousands of years, can never be uprooted.

It was only in the summer of 1927, after Chiang's counterrevolution was well advanced, that the Central Committee tried to take advantage of the peasant movement in Hunan. By that time Moscow was beginning to take notice of the fact that its united front policy in China was running into difficulties. Mao was ordered to establish a Communist régime in Hunan which would be independent of the Kuomintang. But it was too late. The peasants were already too scattered and demoralized to resist the armed might at the disposal of the Kuomintang. Mao's was one of a series of Communist-led peasant uprisings which occurred in September 1927 and are known as the Autumn Harvest Uprisings.

These peasant revolts were intended to reinforce urban insurrections. In the first attempt to establish an urban soviet, Communist forces under Yeh T'ing, Ho Lung, and Chu Teh revolted at Nanchang, the capital of Kiangsi. 1 August, the date of the Nanchang uprising, is celebrated as the anniversary of the establishment of the Chinese Communist army. Forced to flee, Yeh, Ho, and Chu reached the coast in September and occupied Swatow for a week. In the following month they joined with P'eng Pai to establish the first Chinese soviet in the nearby district of Haifeng. In December an attempt was made to establish a Soviet régime at Canton, but the Canton Commune, as it was called, was suppressed with heavy loss of life.

In the spring of 1928 a small force which Chu Teh had extricated from Haifeng joined a band of peasants led by Mao Tse-tung at Chingkangshan, a mountainous area on the Hunan–Kiangsi border. Mao had established himself there the previous October. Chingkangshan was now turned into a soviet base area, and the various units which gathered there became the Fourth Red Army, with Chu as military commander and Mao as political commissar. Up until the establishment of the Chingkangshan soviet, the main object of the insurrections led by the Communists had been to seize cities. It was thought that an entire province could be won once an important city within it had been taken. Mao developed a new strategy based on the concept of rural soviets created in the process of agrarian revolution and defended by armed peasants. Such soviets would initially be situated in remote areas favouring the use of guerrilla tactics by the defenders. Mao found himself in opposition to the Central Committee, which could not bring itself to admit that the countryside could take priority over the cities, for this meant giving priority to the peasants over the proletariat. But the urban revolution had already been smashed: between 1926 and 1930 the proportion of industrial workers in the CCP's membership fell from two-thirds to one-tenth. This was not necessarily tragic, for, as Mao pointed out, in China 'several million industrial workers exist side by side with several hundred million peasants and handicraft workers'. In 1929 Mao and Chu left Chingkangshan for Juichin, located on the southern fringe of Kiangsi, where a new base was created. Other Red units, hardly distinguishable from bandits, were operating in various parts of south China. They gradually coalesced into a number of widely scattered soviets, with Juichin as the 'capital'. Fortified in the mountains, these Communist bases were remarkably resistant to the repeated attacks of Nationalist forces.

Before the Comintern and the CCP Central Committee finally

accepted Mao's verdict on the futility of trying to hold a major city, the Communists launched an extravagant campaign against the Hunanese capital, Changsha, in the summer of 1930. The Red Army was compelled to evacuate the city after occupying it for a week. The Changsha experience, and several ill-fated attempts to seize other towns at about the same time, demonstrated that the CCP's popularity among the urban proletariat was fast waning. All the blame for the Changsha affair was heaped on Li Li-san, who happened to be secretary-general of the Central Committee at the time, just as Li's predecessor, Ch'en Tu-hsiu, had been held responsible for the débâcle of the alliance with the KMT. The way was then clear for the proclamation of the Chinese Soviet Republic at Juichin. Delegates from some 15 soviet areas assembled there on 7 November 1931 for the First All-China Congress of Soviets. A Constitution was adopted and Mao Tse-tung was elected Chairman of the Republic. Chang Kuot'ao, a founding member of the CCP and leader of the large Oyüwan soviet on the borders of Hupei, Honan, and Anhwei provinces, was elected Vice-Chairman. The First Red Army had been created in 1930 out of the units in the Oyüwan soviet. Chu Teh was confirmed in his position of overall Commander-in-Chief of the Red Army.

Five different offensives, each more massive than the one preceding, were launched by Chiang Kai-shek against the Chinese Soviet Republic before it finally succumbed in late 1934. The first three, launched in 1930 and 1931 and employing, respectively, 100,000, 200,000, and 300,000 men, were defeated by a guerrilla strategy then being developed by Mao Tse-tung. The defence of the Soviet area was aided by a moderate land policy, which won the support of a majority of the peasants. At the beginning of 1931, however, a group of 'returned students' from Moscow headed by Wang Ming gained control of the Central Committee. They approached Chinese problems dogmatically, trying to apply the 'correct' Marxist–Leninist theory which they had imbibed in the Soviet Union. They criticized Mao's 'guerrilla' style of war and branded the moderation of the Soviet regime at Juichin as 'rightist'. In fact, they were carrying out a Comintern policy which called for collaboration with fascism against the Western democracies, the same policy which caused the German Communists to undermine socialist opposition to Hitler's rise to power. The 'returned students' evinced no interest in Chinese nationalism but insisted, rather, on a revolutionary struggle exclusively

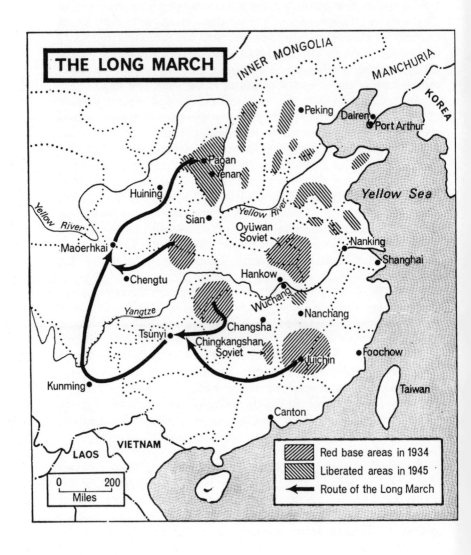

THE LONG MARCH

INNER MONGOLIA

MANCHURIA

KOREA

Peking
Dairen
Port Arthur

Yellow Sea

Paoan
Yenan

Huining

Yellow River

Yellow River

Sian

Oyüwan
Soviet

Nanking

Shanghai

Maoerhkai

Chengtu

Hankow

Wuchang

Nanchang

Yangtze

Changsha

Tsunyi

Chingkangshan
Soviet

Juichin

Foochow

Kunming

Taiwan

Canton

VIETNAM

LAOS

0   200
Miles

▨ Red base areas in 1934

▤ Liberated areas in 1945

◀━ Route of the Long March

on class lines. They ignored the rising tide of criticism in China against Chiang Kai-shek's policy of temporizing in the face of Japanese aggression. By the time of Chiang's fourth annihilation campaign launched in the summer of 1932, this 'sectarian' Central Committee had asserted its authority over Chang Kuo-t'ao and the Oyüwan soviet. The defeat of the Oyüwan soviet by the Nationalists is attributed in official CCP histories to the fact that the First Army employed conventional rather than guerrilla tactics, while Chu's Fourth Army at Juichin defeated the fourth annihilation campaign thanks to its employment of Mao's strategy of avoiding positional warfare. Early in 1933 the 'returned students' had to flee Shanghai and move their Central Committee to Juichin. Rejecting Mao's leadership, they declined to cooperate with a separatist regime which had been set up by a Nationalist splinter group in nearby Fukien, as Mao suggested. Mao's military tactics were also discarded, leading to the defeat of the Fourth Army by the 500,000 Nationalist troops sent against it in the fifth annihilation campaign. This campaign commenced in October 1933 and involved the encirclement and slow strangulation of the Juichin soviet area. Chiang's forces had the help of German advisers and an Anglo-American air arm. After a year's resistance the Mao–Chu forces broke through the Nationalist blockade at the end of 1934 and began the Long March.

The Long March is the epic event of the Chinese Communist revolution. It took a year and covered 6,000 miles. Of the 90,000 men who set out with Mao and Chu, only 20,000 reached their destination, a soviet base area in northern Shensi. The Shensi base, under guerrilla leader Kao Kang, was the last remaining Communist haven in China. Units from other soviet areas subsequently joined them in Shensi. In order to evade pursuing Nationalist troops, a zig-zag course had been followed which led through some of the wildest country in China. At an historic meeting of the Politburo of the Central Committee at Tsunyi, Kweichow, in January 1935, the returned students were forced to acquiesce in the leadership of Mao Tse-tung, who was elected Chairman of the Central Committee. Another important Central Committee meeting was held during the Long March. It was convened at Maoerhkai, Szechwan, following the linking up of Mao's Fourth Army and the First Army under Chang Kuo-t'ao in July 1935. The conference issued a proclamation on 1 August calling for a united front of all classes to fight against Japanese aggression.

The Sian Incident

While his best troops were trying to exterminate the Communists in the south, Chiang Kai-shek's response to the Mukden Incident of 18 September 1931 was to turn the whole problem of Japanese aggression in Manchuria over to the League of Nations. The Report of the Lytton Commission, which had been sent to Manchuria by the League, condemned Japanese aggression; no effective sanctions were imposed, however. Thus, Japan was able to maintain the artificial state of Manchukuo which it had created in March 1932 with the former Ch'ing emperor, Henry Pu-yi, as chief executive. Isolated acts of resistance on the part of Chinese commanders did occur, but they were not authorized by the Nanking government. Manchuria's great warlord, Chang Hsüeh-liang, was in China with half his troops, and Chiang Kai-shek advised him to stay there. In general, the petty warlords of Manchuria were not greatly discomfited by the establishment of Manchukuo, while the masses were politically passive. In Shanghai and other cities of China, however, the Japanese aggression provoked demonstrations, strikes, and boycotts, all of which were clearly anti-Japanese. Only ten days after the Mukden Incident, students in Nanking beat the minister of foreign affairs to emphasize their dissatisfaction with the government's failure to declare war. The Communists tried to capitalize on this sentiment by issuing a declaration of war against Japan from their Soviet Republic at Juichin in April 1932.

The Japanese next struck at Shanghai, where a student-led boycott had brought Japanese business practically to a standstill. At midnight on 28-29 January the Japanese launched their attack from the International Settlement. They fell upon Chapei, the heart of the Chinese section of the city. Attacking with 4,000 marines, the Japanese apparently expected to punish the Chinese citizenry for their anti-Japanese behaviour and then withdraw. But due to the unexpected resistance of the 19th Route Army under Ts'ai T'ing-kai, the Japanese were still fighting a month later, by which time they had committed 30,000 men. The 19th Route Army had participated in the Northern Expedition after having received training from Soviet officers at Canton. It was not an entirely trustworthy unit from Chiang's point of view, and he disapproved of its defence of Shanghai. However, the enthusiastic support of the local people, who volunteered their labour as well as their savings, made the 19th largely independent of Nanking. Japanese bombing of the Chinese community and use of Chinese prisoners for bayonet practice became routine. Popular feeling ran so high that Chiang had to send reinforcements, but the build-up of Japanese troops finally obliged the defenders to withdraw from the city. The 34-day war at Shanghai was terminated by a humiliating settlement in which the Nationalist government undertook to stop the anti-Japanese agitation, which had become nation-wide. Even so, the Shanghai venture had turned into a costly fiasco for the Japanese, and several admirals were recalled to Tokyo during the fighting. Henceforth, Tokyo concentrated on China's northern provinces, far from the prying eyes of foreigners and from the Communist-inspired élan which pervaded the Cantonese troops of the 19th Route Army. Chiang's persistent policy of appeasement finally caused the 19th to go into open revolt in October 1933, when it set up a short-lived people's government in Fukien.

Opposition to Chiang Kai-shek also developed in Canton, where a breakaway regime comprising Kwangtung and Kwangsi provinces and calling itself the South-west Political Council demanded that Chiang deal more firmly with Japan. This demand was echoed by the bourgeois press in Shanghai. Chiang was finding it as difficult to control the populace as Tokyo was to control its admirals and generals. It is likely that there had been an informal understanding between Chiang and Tokyo for spheres of influence in China which was now being made unworkable by the twin forces of Japanese militarism and Chinese patriotism.

In the north, Feng Yü-hsiang organized an Anti-Japanese Allied Army in May 1933 for the protection of Chahar province in Inner Mongolia. In February the Japanese had overrun the province of Jehol, which lay between Manchuria and Chahar. Though more costly than the Mukden fighting of September 1931, the Japanese campaign in Jehol was scarcely opposed. The mixture of warlord and central government troops theoretically defending Jehol simply melted away before Japan's mechanized columns. The Manchurian troops of Chang Hsüeh-liang, which comprised the bulk of the defenders, had been left badly demoralized by the Mukden Incident, when they had remained idle south of the Great Wall. Troops of the local warlord, T'ang Yü-lin, whom Nanking had made provincial governor of Jehol, went over to the Japanese in large numbers. Only half of the invading force had been made up of Japanese troops even when it entered Jehol: the rest were Chinese auxiliaries, puppet Manchukuo troops. Whereas the contemporaneous attack on Shanghai provoked a patriotic outcry, Japan encountered no national resistance to its ten-day conquest of Jehol, which left the vast, snow-covered mountains of the province littered with the bodies of Chinese soldiers. Scarcely pausing at the Great Wall, the Japanese forces continued south from Jehol. They easily pushed back government forces under Ho Ying-ch'in, Nanking's Minister of War, until they occupied much of Hopei and threatened the province's two great cities, Peking and Tientsin. In line with the government's policy of 'resist but don't fight' vis-à-vis Japan, Ho brought hostilities to an end by an agreement signed on 31 May 1933. The Tangku Truce regularized the Japanese seizure of Jehol by creating south and west of it, along the Great Wall, a demilitarized zone from which all forces considered hostile to Japan were to be withdrawn, while Japan undertook to withdraw its own forces from Hopei. Nanking thereupon requested Feng Yü-hsiang's troops to give up their resistance to the Japanese and quit Chahar.

In the months following the Tangku Truce relations between China proper and Manchuria were regularized to the point of constituting *de facto* recognition of Manchukuo by Nanking. Tokyo raised the stakes in the following year, however, by an official government statement of 17 April 1934 which sought to establish a sort of Japanese Monroe Doctrine for China and East Asia. Nanking still tried to negotiate. In June 1935 General Ho Ying-ch'in reached an understanding with General Umetsu Yishijiro concerning the demilitarization of Chahar and Hopei. Nanking also committed itself, through the Ho–Umetsu Agreement, to prohibit all anti-Japanese agitation in China. The Japanese followed this up with an attempt to carve out a puppet state in north China which would embrace Shantung, Hopei, Shansi, Chahar, and Suiyuan. At the same time, smuggling from Manchuria down through north China all the way to the Yangtze reached such proportions as to reduce the maritime customs collected at Shanghai. Narcotics, as well as ordinary merchandise, were pouring into north China. Galled by this trend of affairs, the students of Peking staged mass demonstrations on 9 December and 16 December 1935. Though harried by squads of Blue Shirts, Chiang's fascist-type gendarmerie, and censored out of the national press, the December Ninth movement helped to forestall Japan in her attempt to take all of north China by diplomacy and it contributed to the mounting pressure on Nanking for a united front against Japan.

In December 1936 Chiang Kai-shek flew to Sian, Shensi, to find out why Chang Hsüeh-liang was not pressing forward with a new offensive against the Communists in the northern part of the province, as ordered by Nanking. In a sensational development which became known as the Sian Incident, Chiang was arrested and detained for 14 days, during which time his Manchurian host implored him to abandon his attempt to destroy the Communists before fighting the Japanese ('pacification within, then resistance without'), but rather to work with the Communists in an anti-Japanese united front. Chou En-lai, a former colleague of Chiang's at Whampoa, arrived from the Communist headquarters at nearby Paoan to add his arguments to Chang's. The Communists had come out in favour of a united-front policy in the previous year, and in the meantime they had demonstrated to Chang Hsüeh-liang that they could not be easily suppressed. In November 1936 the country was thrilled by a Chinese victory at Pailingmiao, where central government troops under General Fu Tso-yi routed a superior Japanese force, thereby blocking their advance into Suiyuan province, north of Shensi. Nevertheless, Chiang was not readily convinced. Only when his captors made it clear that he would not leave Sian alive unless he concurred, and when Madame Chiang flew to Sian to add her pleas to those of Chang and Chou, did the President of China finally give in to the demand that the country be defended. Chiang was released on Christmas Day. Although the militarists in the Nanking government were disgruntled at this turn of events, Chiang's new policy had the support of the pro-American faction. When he returned to the capital, he was accompanied by Chang Hsüeh-liang, who personified the united-front policy. The Sian Incident made Chiang a national hero. Suddenly, his leadership was acclaimed on all sides, and the various factions which had challenged his authority now broke off their opposition. Had Chiang made a different decision at Sian, Ho Ying-ch'in and the other Japanese-oriented generals at Nanking would probably have cooperated with Japan in her project to make China a colony. During Chiang's captivity these generals had made contact with Wang Ching-wei, the logical head of a puppet Chinese government, who had just seen Hitler in Berlin.

On the night of 7–8 July 1937 an incident occurred at the Marco Polo Bridge outside Peking, in which shots were exchanged between Chinese and Japanese troops. The latter had been holding provocative manoeuvres in the area. The incident was no more serious than others which had been smoothed over in previous years. But this time there were no negotiations: the Sino–Japanese War had begun.

Literature

The outstanding writer of the Literary Revolution, and, indeed, of twentieth-century China, was Lu Hsün (pseudonym of Chou Shujen, 1881–1936). His short story, 'A Madman's Diary', was the first modern work of fiction to appear in China. It was written in the vernacular (*pai-hua*) and published in the April 1918 issue of *New Youth*, the magazine which helped to stimulate the May Fourth movement. 'A Madman's Diary' is a scathing attack on Confucianism, which Lu Hsün depicts as a specious morality used to disguise a man-eating social system. In other stories, most of them written before 1926, Lu Hsün continued to expose the old society's suppression or destruction of the individual. Russian realism, and especially the works of Maxim Gorky, had a strong influence on Lu Hsün's stories, which nevertheless have a distinctly Chinese flavour. The best-known is 'The True Story of Ah Q' (1921). Ah Q is an illiterate, landless labourer, who is always getting a beating, being unjustly fined, or losing his job; but he manages each time to win a 'moral victory' by discovering that in some way he is more of a Confucian gentleman than his tormentors. While ridiculing Ah Q, Lu Hsün also shows compassion for him, but not for the hypocritical gentry whose moral standards Ah Q tries to imitate, and who are responsible for his imprisonment for a crime he did not commit. Ah Q is shot by soldiers of the 1911 Revolution, his execution intended to inspire the people with awe of the new regime. The soldiers use foreign rifles. Here Lu Hsün is attacking imported as well as traditional values, for by the early 1920s Western ideas and forms were being uncritically adopted by many of his fellow intellectuals, as well as by the bourgeoisie.

In 1921 *New Youth* was closed down by the police in the French Concession in Shanghai. Those who had been associated with the magazine split into three groups. The leftists, led by Ch'en Tu-hsiu, turned from cultural pursuits to politics, while the rightists, among them Hu Shih, withdrew from the Literary Revolution and devoted themselves to critical, scientific re-appraisal of China's cultural heritage. Most of those who continued to make writing their main activity comprised a middle group. Uncommitted politically, they hoped that somehow love, beauty, and humanitarianism would triumph in a China freed of its feudal heritage. Some of these *pai-hua* writers founded the Literary Research Society in 1921. Its purpose was to promote realism, 'art for life's sake': Mao Tun (pen-name of Shen Yen-ping), its most prominent member and editor of its magazine, *The Short Story*, declared that literature should 'awaken the masses and give them strength'.

The next year a group of students who had returned from Japan and were disappointed by conditions in China founded the Creation Society, dedicated to self-expression and 'art to beautify life'. Yü Ta-fu's stories of personal dissatisfaction and sexual frustration, and Kuo Mo-jo's impassioned, romantic poems and plays were representative of the output of this group. However, Kuo and other members of the Creation Society soon turned to Marxism. 'Romantic literature', Kuo wrote in 1926, 'has become counterrevolutionary literature, whereas socialist literature is realistic literature, the newest and most progressive revolutionary literature of our age.' In an article entitled 'From Literary Revolution to Revolutionary Literature', another Creationist, Ch'eng Fang-wu, denounced political neutralism in literature.

The 1927 Kuomintang–Communist split polarized Chinese writers into left and right camps. Hounded out of Kuomintang areas, the leftists congregated in Shanghai. While some produced pessimistic novels and stories about their recent revolutionary experiences, there was a growing trend to add anti-imperialism and class struggle to the older theme of anti-feudalism, to try to adopt the language and outlook of the masses, and to depict workers and peasants as militant rather than passive. Lu Hsün—who now wrote mainly brief, topical essays—criticized this 'proletarian literature' movement for not really being literature of the masses 'because the masses have not yet opened their lips'. But in 1928–30 he translated Soviet works on literary theory and he was instrumental in founding the League of Left-Wing Writers in March 1930. Declaring that 'we must stand in the front line of the proletariat's struggle for liberation', the League undertook to promote proletarian literature and Marxist theories on art. The reading public, sated with romance and self-expression, welcomed fiction dealing with economic realities, such as Mao Tun's story, *Spring Silkworms* (1932), about peasants hit by the world depression.

In response to Japan's attacks on China and to the shifting Comintern line, the League of Left-Wing Writers changed itself into the

Anti-Japanese United Front of Writers and Artists in 1936, a few months before Chiang Kai-shek committed himself to fighting the Japanese. Henceforth, patriotism and resistance were the themes favoured by both Communist and Kuomintang writers. Left-wing writers could now leave Shanghai. Those who went to Yenan came increasingly under the influence of official CCP ideas of what and how they should write. The problem of literature was considered by Mao Tse-tung himself as part of his wide-ranging re-interpretation of the Chinese revolution. His 'Talks at the Yenan Forum on Literature and Art', delivered in May 1942, were to become the basis of literary orthodoxy in the People's Republic of China. 'Literature and art are subordinate to politics', he said, but they are 'an indispensable part of the entire revolutionary cause'. Since 'all literature and art belong to definite classes', Communist writers must renounce their own petty-bourgeois individualism and—by means of practical revolutionary work and the study of Marxism and society—shift their stand to that of the working masses. Although political criteria come first, artistic quality must not be neglected. It was still permissible to expose the backward, feudal aspects of society, but pessimism was now incorrect; writers must emphasize the 'bright side'—the successes won by the workers and peasants in their revolutionary struggle under the leadership of the CCP.

CHAPTER FOUR

War and Civil War

The Sino-Japanese War

To underscore his determination to resist Japan, Chiang signed a non-aggression pact with the Soviet Union, the only power prepared to give more than vocal assistance to Nanking. In the two years following signature of the pact on 21 August 1937, Moscow extended credits of US $250 million to the Nationalist government. Soviet supplies reached China by ship from the Black Sea until October 1938, when, with the capture of Canton, the Japanese were able to blockade the China coast; thereafter, they were trucked into China's north-west via Sinkiang. Soviet fighter planes, with their pilots, were dispatched to help defend Chinese cities against Japanese air attack. Soviet advisers were also sent, some of them veterans of the earlier period of collaboration with Sun Yat-sen. The most important figure in the impressive Soviet military mission which came to China in 1938 was General Grigori K. Zhukov. The following year found Zhukov at Nomonhan, on the frontier between Manchuria and Outer Mongolia, fending off probes by Japan's aggressive Kwantung Army. A major battle developed during the summer of 1939, turning into a virtual undeclared war. In the end the Japanese suffered a stunning defeat, with 18,000 killed or wounded. The tactics as well as the equipment of the Japanese had been found wanting by comparison with those of the combined Mongol–Soviet force under Zhukov. The battle of Nomonhan demonstrated that Japan's entire war machine in China was dangerously exposed to flanking attack. Until the Soviet–Japanese Non-Aggression Pact of April 1941, therefore, the Soviet military forces poised in Siberia and Mongolia served as a check on Japanese ambitions in China.

The Western democracies were slow to react to the Sino–Japanese War, except negatively. In 1937, in order to avoid complications with Japan, the United States abjectly withdrew the infantry regiment which it had maintained at Tientsin under the Boxer Protocol, leaving behind in China only a few detachments of marines to guard American lives and property. The Americans, who did not have a concession of their own, had made use of the British Concession in Tientsin. It was now subjected to increasing Japanese harassment. Japan's invasion of China exposed the feebleness of the American and British military position in the Far East, thus making it impossible for Washington or London to play an important political role in the conflict. They struck poses which failed to impress the Japanese. At the Brussels Conference, held at the instigation of the US and the League of Nations in November 1937 to consider the crisis in China, only Litvinov, the Soviet Foreign Minister, could urge positive action. He got little response. Even the Japanese attacks on the USS *Panay* and HMS *Ladybird* in the Yangtze River in December 1937 failed to arouse the American and British publics.

During 1938 a million Chinese were mobilized to complete the Burma Road. Built entirely with primitive tools, it ran through the rugged mountains between Kunming, capital of Yunnan province in south-west China, and the railhead at Lashio in north Burma. This feat, which US Army engineers had said was impossible, opened a second back door for China, supplementing the Soviet-built road in the north-west. Supplies began reaching China via the Burma Road at the beginning of 1939 after the US and Britain, responding to Japan's proclamation of its New Order in East Asia, extended credits to the Nationalist government. Though small in comparison with Soviet credits, these loans, of $25 million and £450,000, signified Anglo–American determination not to abandon Chiang Kai-shek. Britain wavered in the following year, however, when Tokyo insisted that it recognize Japan's New Order or suffer the consequences. British investments in China were far larger than American investments. The understanding reached between Ambassador Craigie and Foreign Minister Arita was announced in Tokyo on 24 July 1939. To let the Japanese know that the US, notwithstanding the British move, had not altered its own course, Secretary of State Cordell Hull on 26 July denounced the American–Japanese commercial treaty of 1911; suspension of trade relations would become effective six months later. When it became apparent that the Nationalist government was not prepared to come to terms, Tokyo set up a puppet Chinese government in March 1940 and, in the hope of securing its position in Asia against a possible challenge from the US, entered into the Tripartite Pact with Berlin and Rome in September of the same year.

In the actual fighting, the Japanese soon succeeded in occupying north China, the Yangtze valley, and the ports on the south-east coast. Immediately following the outbreak of hostilities at the Marco Polo Bridge on 7 July 1937, the Japanese had cleared defending forces from Peking and Tientsin, capturing both cities by the end of July. As reinforcements poured in from Manchuria, the Japanese advanced westward from the Peking area. In mid-October they captured Paotow, at the terminus of the Peking–Suiyuan railway. By 8 November the Chinese had been forced to give up Taiyuan, capital of Shansi province. In the east, the Shantung cities of Tsinan and Tsingtao were captured in December. By the end of 1937, therefore, the Japanese controlled the principal cities and lines of communication in north China.

Meanwhile, hostilities were under way in the Yangtze valley. Whereas Chinese resistance in the north had been uncoordinated and generally ineffective, a determined stand was made at Shanghai. The incident which touched off the fighting in the Shanghai area was the shooting on 9 August of two Japanese marines by a sentry at a Chinese airfield. The fighting continued through September, October, and November before the Japanese succeeded in out-flanking and breaking the Chinese resistance. By committing his best troops to this battle, Chiang Kai-shek won international recognition of China's determination to resist Japanese aggression, but on strictly military grounds it was wasteful. Nanking as well as Shanghai had to be abandoned by the end of December. Due to the terrible atrocities committed by Japanese troops, their seizure of the Chinese capital is often referred to as 'the rape of Nanking'.

During 1938 the war was distinguished by a Japanese defeat, their most serious thus far, at Taierhchwang, near the Shantung–Kiangsu border, on 7 April. The Nationalist troops which won the day at Taierhchwang belonged to the Kwangsi armies of Li Tsung-jen and Pai Chung-hsi, the men who had earlier broken with Nanking for its failure to fight the Japanese. The Japanese soon regained the initiative, however, and began moving westward across north China. In June the retreating Nationalists, with an almost unbelievable disregard for the lives of China's rural population, employed artillery to breach the dykes of the Yellow River in an effort to check the Japanese advance. The breaching of the dykes, which caused a great flood and changed the course of the river for years to come, succeeded in temporarily preventing the loss of Chengchow, an important rail centre in Honan province.

Hankow, which had become the Nationalist capital following the loss of Nanking, was captured by the Japanese on 25 October 1938. Chiang Kai-shek's government was obliged to seek refuge further upstream, behind the Yangtze gorges, in Szechwan. Chungking, the chief city of the province, remained the Nationalist capital for the duration of the war. The fall of Hankow marked the beginning of a period of military stalemate during which the Japanese tried unsuccessfully to capture Changsha, gateway to south China, and wrestled with the guerrillas who operated behind their lines in north China. During 1939, however, the south China coastal cities of Amoy and Swatow, as well as the island of Hainan, were taken by the Japanese in seaborne attacks. This enabled them to consolidate their blockade of the south China coast, which had begun with the capture of Canton in the previous year. Following the fall of France in 1940, the Japanese blockade was extended to China's overland routes with Indochina, while the British authorities were pressured into closing the Burma Road from July to October 1940. Two years later Burma fell (to the Japanese) and the road was closed for good. Thereafter, China's main link with the outside world was by air over 'the hump' to India.

Chungking and Yenan

As a result of the Sino–Japanese War, the monopoly of power which the Nationalists had previously enjoyed in China was broken. The Nationalists were never able to regain their lost position, which had rested on a three-way alliance of landed wealth, military force, and urban capital. This alliance could not be reconstituted after the Japanese were swept from the scene in 1945 because the peasants which it had oppressed had in the meantime been mobilized by the Communists. Armed and awakened, the peasant masses could not be made to accept a return to the old order of things. The Japanese had indeed brought a 'new order' to China, but not the one they had intended. Paradoxically, their occupation of the country made possible the very Communist victory which they were allegedly seeking to prevent.

Abandonment of the lower Yangtze valley by the Nationalists in the initial stages of the war cut them off from Shanghai, the financial centre of the nation. Loss of receipts from the Maritime Customs, as well as from most ordinary taxes, was a heavy blow to the Kuomintang, and when it adopted the expediency of simply printing more paper money to cover its expenditures the result was runaway inflation. The severing of connections between the Nationalist government and foreign banks was acknowledged by Chungking in 1939 when it announced that it could no longer meet its obligations under existing international loans. Chiang Kai-shek's flight into the interior also had serious political consequences, for it virtually detached the Generalissimo from the moderate wing of the Kuomintang, represented by the Westernized bourgeoisie, and drove him into a closer relationship with the Party's most reactionary elements. Szechwan was the home ground of the notorious Chen brothers, warlords Chen Li-fu and Chen Kuo-fu, from whom the 'CC Clique' took its name. Chiang had brought the Chen brothers into the Nationalist fold prior to his anti-Communist coup of 1927; their support was a necessary precondition for his seizure of Shanghai. Once isolated in Szechwan, Chiang no longer had sufficient support from other factions to counterbalance the CC clique. During the war the CC clique supported the increasingly dictatorial role which Chiang assumed with respect to all moderate elements within the Kuomintang. Under Chiang, the CC Clique shared effective power only with the military faction, or Whampoa clique. There was no meaningful participation in government by the people, and the civil and military bureaucracy, from Chiang's close relatives on down, was rife with corruption.

From the Nationalist point of view, the united front with the Communists had been predicated on the assumption of a quick war against Japan. It was thought that a spirited resistance on the part of Nanking would oblige the Japanese to negotiate, and that a reasonable settlement would be possible. Despite protracted efforts by German mediators, however, terms acceptable to Chiang Kai-shek could not be wrung from the Japanese. But a Kuomintang splinter group led by Wang Ching-wei, abandoning Chiang to his exile in Chungking, formed a Nanking government under Japanese control. The establishment of the Wang Ching-wei regime meant that Japan could forego indefinitely a final solution to the 'China question' posed by the Chungking government while it proceeded with the building of its New Order in East Asia. The refusal of Washington and Moscow to withdraw recognition from Chungking was denounced by Tokyo, but was not enough to deflect the Japanese from their course. These developments put an entirely different complexion on the KMT–CCP alliance, which had seemed comparatively harmless in the autumn of 1937.

By an agreement signed 22 September 1937, approximately midway in time between the Marco Polo Bridge incident and the fall of Nanking, the Nationalists officially recognized the existence of the CCP's army and area of control centered on Yenan, Shensi. This agreement gave substance to the understanding reached at Sian the previous December. The CCP agreed to drop the designations 'Soviet' and 'Red Army' in favour of the more innocuous 'Border Region government' and 'Eighth Route Army'. In principle, the Communists were incorporated both militarily and administratively into the Nationalist regime, and Chiang actually transmitted funds for their support. The Eighth Route Army, commanded by Chu Teh, proceeded forthwith to engage the Japanese in the north. Later in the year the New Fourth Army was organized. Its area of operations was the lower Yangtze valley. Employing the guerrilla tactics they had developed years before in the defence of their Soviet areas against Nationalist attack, the Eighth Route and New Fourth Armies operated behind the Japanese lines with remarkable success. They remained after Chiang's conventional forces had retired behind the mountain barriers of western China. The ability of Communist power to survive in areas nominally controlled by the Japanese confronted Chiang Kai-shek with a dilemma: if he undertook offensive operations against the Japanese he would simply be wasting resources which he would need in the ultimate contest with the Communists, yet to remain passively on the defensive was to abandon the field to the Communists. He added a second negative policy to the one already being pursued: while continuing to stand on the defensive vis-à-vis the Japanese, he now tried to neutralize Yenan and paralyse its military operations by means of a blockade. Meanwhile, such war material as the Soviet Union and the United States would send him was husbanded for the civil war with the Communists which Chiang knew would follow Japan's defeat by the Allies.

As had been the case during the first united front (1924–27), Communist strength increased rapidly during the second KMT–CCP alliance, beginning in 1937. By 1940 the Communist armies were ten times as large as they had been at the outbreak of the Sino–

Japanese War and they had established effective local government over a large part of north China. The more the Japanese struggled to root out the Communists, the more their power grew. A 'three-all' policy—kill all, destroy all, burn all—was employed by the Japanese in their campaigns against rural areas thought to support guerrillas. The ruthlessness of the Japanese was such as to fill even the passive north China peasant with anger. In 1939 Chungking instituted its blockade of Yenan: for this purpose a line of 10,000 fortified block-houses was constructed and 200,000 of Chiang's best troops deployed. The pattern of the early 1930s, when the pick of Nanking's troops had been thrown against the Chinese Soviet Republic while the Japanese took over Manchuria, was being repeated. Clearly, Chiang considered the Communists to be the primary enemy.

Insofar as it constituted an effective alliance, the second united front was brought to an end in January 1941 when elements of the New Fourth Army were attacked by Chiang's troops. This was a far more serious affair than the minor clashes between Communist and Nationalist forces which had been occurring since 1939. The Communist representatives in the Nationalist civilian and military hier-archies returned to Yenan, and there was no further cooperation between the CCP and the KMT.

Despite the Nationalist blockade, conditions in Yenan were better than in Chungking. Comparative abundance and equitable distribu-tion of food; development of handicraft industries; stable currency; honesty and frugality of officials—these were some of the factors which made popular morale so much higher in the Communist area than in areas of Nationalist control. The Communists were experi-menting with reforms that would eventually be instituted all over China, while the Nationalists were vainly trying to prop themselves up with archaic usages and outmoded patterns of thought and be-haviour, as rationalized in Chiang Kai-shek's 1943 book, *China's Destiny*. The civilian and military organization of the Nationalists had a modern veneer, but it was rotten inside. The Communist exterior was quaint, but its content was revolutionary.

The emergence of Maoism

In the quiet of Yenan, behind the double blockade of Kuomintang and Japanese troops, Mao Tse-tung devoted himself to the task of grafting Marxist–Leninist theory on to the base of peasant revolt. He knew that a peasant rebellion of the old style could no longer succeed in China because the forces of reaction in the countryside had been reinforced by urban commercial interests which had the support of foreign powers. Only a thoroughgoing, modern revolution which would sweep away at one time landlord, bureaucrat-capitalist, and imperialist would suffice. China had to free itself of its semi-colonial status as well as its own backwardness; the Chinese revolution had to be national as well as social. The Chinese revolution could not succeed alone, but would have to be part of the world revolution led by the Soviet Union. Classical Marxism–Leninism held that, in any particular country, the bourgeois revolution against feudalism would produce a national state based on capitalism, which would in turn be displaced by a proletarian revolution. But a revolution in a colonial country could be neither of these. It had to be both at the same time: an anti-feudal, anti-capitalist revolution occurring within the anti-imperialist context established by the October Revolution. Contrary to the views held by Lenin and Stalin in the 1920s, it would not lead to the foundation of a capitalist or a socialist state, but to a 'new democratic' state. The capitalist stage would be by-passed, and the revolution could evolve peacefully from the stage of new democracy to the stage of socialism.

On New Democracy, published in 1940, is one of Mao's most original and important works. It provided the theoretical framework for the revolutionary techniques, or methods, which the CCP would employ: in the military realm, guerrilla warfare; in the political realm, the united front; in the economic realm, land reform. Mao devoted a great deal of attention to military doctrine. An effective army was a prerequisite for the survival and the expansion of the Soviet area. Drawing on his own experience, as well as on the writings of the classical Chinese military thinker, Sun Tzu, and the pattern of earlier Chinese rebellions, Mao produced a plan for victory on the battlefield. In his celebrated 'Problems of Strategy in Guerrilla War Against Japan' and 'On Protracted War', both dating from 1938, Mao emphasized a war of movement which would enable the guerrilla forces to pounce on isolated units of the enemy and gradually exhaust him. Since China is a large country, the enemy would be obliged to disperse his forces over a wide area, and this would make it possible for the guerrillas, though far weaker than the enemy in total strength, to achieve local superiority. Since the Communists had the support of the peasants, the guerrillas were at home among them, 'like fish in water', but the countryside was inhospitable to the enemy.

Fortified in the cities and strung out over long lines of communication, the enemy was always visible and subject to surprise attack; if he tried to attack the guerrillas, they melted away; if he took reprisals against the rural population he only produced more recruits for the guerrillas. Eventually the guerrillas would be able to assume the strategic offensive and, employing conventional tactics, eliminate the fortified positions of the enemy.

The idea of a broad, patriotic united front against Japan appealed to all classes in China, was an acute embarrassment to Chiang Kai-shek, and answered the requirements of Comintern policy. It had a special appeal for Mao, who observed in 1935 that Japanese aggression, by taking over all the positions of influence previously held by the various powers, had converted the status of China from that of 'a semi-colony shared by several powers to that of a colony of Japan alone'. Participation in a patriotic war of resistance against Japan would facilitate the expansion of CCP power territorially and enable it to gain multi-class influence. Mao was careful to insist, however, that there would be no repetition of the 'bloc within' which had proved so disastrous in the first united front, of 1924–27. In the second united front the CCP and its peasant base would remain a 'bloc without'. The CCP would gladly cooperate with all genuinely patriotic forces, but would not again subject itself to external control. In the administration of liberated areas, political power would be wielded by 'the people', comprising the peasants and other revolutionary classes. In his 1945 report, 'On Coalition Government', Mao spelled out the conditions under which a joint CCP–KMT government could be set up after the defeat of Japan and civil war be avoided.

Apart from the idea of an all-powerful Communist Party, there was little in Marxism–Leninism that survived the revision of it by Mao Tse-tung at Yenan. Mao adopted without substantial modification the Leninist party organization based on a pyramidal cellular structure and the operational technique of 'democratic centralism'. Democratic centralism meant the participation of all Party members in the decision-making process, but strict discipline at all Party echelons once a decision had been reached. But Mao introduced an important dynamic element to maintain the revolutionary élan of Party members. This was the concept of criticism and self-criticism of individual members, and the parallel concept of rectification of the Party or parts of it. Unlike the Russians, the Chinese comrades did not have a static concept of individual and group behaviour: an individual or a group could be re-educated. Liquidation was only necessary in exceptional cases. The first large-scale rectification campaign of the CCP was launched in 1942 at Yenan in order to raise the ideological level of peasant members from the newly-liberated rural areas and of middle-class members from enemy-occupied urban areas. Of no less importance was the need to convert to Maoism those members of the Party who were excessively loyal to the CPSU.

Through the Maoism that emerged from the Yenan period the CCP experienced a rebirth. The subservience to Moscow that had characterized the Party since its foundation was ended. Mao, the Hunanese school teacher and peasant leader who had never been abroad nor learned a foreign language, had snatched control of the Party out of the hands of the Westernized, alienated intellectuals and given it a pungently Chinese stamp. He had led the Party through the Long March, out of defeat to the threshold of victory, and had emerged as just the sort of hero that Mao himself had read about in his youth. Now, in Yenan, Mao had endowed the CCP with an ideological personality of its own. He had sinified Marxism–Leninism and created a new belief system for Chinese intellectuals who had sampled all the 'isms' the West had to offer and come away unsatisfied. Maoism provided a structure around which a new China could be built, and they flocked to its standard. This was important, because, as Mao well knew, no peasant revolution had ever succeeded in China which did not have the support of the intelligentsia.

China as an ally of the USA, the USSR, and the UK

In the Second World War, as in the First, China waited for the US position to be clarified before making a decision of its own. Although in both cases China imitated the US, issuing a declaration of war against Germany and her associates, it showed a degree of sympathy for Berlin which suggests that the Chinese were simply waiting until the outcome of the conflict could be foreseen before taking sides. As militarists, both Yüan Shih-k'ai and Chiang Kai-shek had a profound respect for the German military tradition, and their impatience with parliamentary government did not predispose them to join the Anglo–American camp. Chiang retained his pro-German sentiments until the Battle of Stalingrad in the winter of 1942–43 made the eventual Nazi defeat less uncertain than it had been up until that point in the war. Chiang's equivocation was the more remarkable inasmuch as

China had been fighting an undeclared war with Germany's partner, Japan, since 1937.

Nevertheless, President Roosevelt evinced a huge enthusiasm for Generalissimo and Madame Chiang Kai-shek from the moment the two countries became allies. Ignoring the fact that the Nationalist government had displayed no appetite whatsoever for hostilities since retiring to Chungking three years earlier, Washington rushed to make China one of the Big Four. Churchill and Stalin went along, although the latter consistently refused to participate in any meeting attended by Chiang. The British had never warmed to the Kuomintang, as the Americans had, and Anglo–Chinese relations did not improve during the war. The Russians, who had been China's most important ally during the Sino–Japanese War (1937–41), had lost interest in Chungking after 1938, when it became obvious that Chiang was prepared to launch offensive operations only against the Communists. Britain joined the United States and other states in formally renouncing, on 11 January 1943, their rights of extra-territoriality in China; the Soviet Union had done so 20 years earlier. Formal liquidation of the remaining foreign concessions in China was achieved at the same time, but this move did not affect the status of the Crown Colony of Hong Kong, which remained British. All these areas were under Japanese occupation at the time, so that the powers were graciously giving back to China something they no longer possessed. Moreover, China's wartime allies promised that Manchuria and Formosa would be returned to China following the defeat of Japan. Thanks to strong American pressure, China was promised a permanent seat in the United Nations Security Council.

Without having made any positive contribution to the war effort, Chungking had thus derived very substantial advantages, including great-power status, from its declaration of war on the Axis powers. Its principal contribution was a negative one: owing to China's refusal to capitulate, more Japanese troops had to be kept in the country than would otherwise have been necessary. The participation of Chinese troops in the Burma campaign of 1944–45, under the overall command of China's American military adviser, General Joseph W. Stilwell, was also a net gain for Chungking, since the troops in question were completely retrained and re-equipped, while the campaign itself had no discernible influence on the course of the war. Also advantageous for Chungking was the stationing of the 14th US Air Force in south China. Its activities helped to sustain

American interest in the China theatre, and at the war's end its aircraft and supplies were turned over to the Nationalist government.

Damage inflicted on their troops, planes, and lines of communication in China by the 14th Air Force was one reason for the Japanese summer offensive of 1944. This was their first major offensive since 1938, and it was to be their last of the war. Employing units transferred from Manchuria, the Japanese offensive thrust southward from the Yangtze valley along the Hankow–Canton and Hunan–Kwangsi railways, opening up a land route to Indochina and isolating the south-east coast of China from the interior provinces. By November the Americans were forced to pull back from the forward air-bases which had become such an irritation to the Japanese. The 1944 offensive also revealed the extent to which the Nationalist armies had deteriorated during the years of military inactivity, for the Japanese encountered only sporadic and disorganized resistance.

On 9 August 1945 the Soviet Union declared war on Japan. By the 15th, the date of Japan's surrender to the United Nations, Soviet troops occupied key positions throughout Manchuria. A Sino-Soviet Treaty of Friendship and Alliance had been signed on the previous day, 14 August. During July Foreign Ministers T. V. Soong and V. M. Molotov had held discussions in Moscow on the terms of this treaty, which served to ratify decisions reached at Yalta without Chinese participation. In return for its entry into the war against Japan, the Soviet Union was to regain its sphere of influence in Manchuria, lost in 1905 as a result of the Russo-Japanese War.The treaty called for joint Sino-Soviet operation of the Chinese Eastern and South Manchurian Railroads and guaranteed the Soviet Union use of Port Arthur and Dairen. However, all Soviet troops were to be withdrawn from Manchuria at an early date. Harsh as these terms may have appeared at a time when the special rights of other powers in China were being liquidated, the 1945 Sino-Soviet treaty was really a triumph for Chungking. The Nationalists were lucky enough to have Manchuria restored to them at all. The real importance of the treaty was that by means of it Chiang Kai-shek gained Moscow's neutrality in the forthcoming Chinese civil war. On the whole, Moscow faithfully carried out its pledge to recognize only the Nationalist government and to abstain from any interference in China's internal affairs. The record of the United States government was less innocent.

General Stilwell was recalled from China in October 1944 when it became impossible for him any longer to work with Generalissimo Chiang Kai-shek, whom he was supposed to advise on military matters. His mission had been, on behalf of Washington, to energize Chungking's war effort and to see that the best possible use was made of American lend-lease supplies. Friction arose between the two men because Stilwell perceived—and demonstrated by his effective use of Chinese troops in Burma—that the Nationalist armies were incapacitated by a military and government bureaucracy so corrupt, incompetent, and despotic that only the most radical measures could meet the situation. Chiang retorted that the strength of the nation was being sapped by the Communists, and that until they were dealt with the war against Japan could not be vigorously prosecuted. Roosevelt was at first sympathetic with Stilwell's recommendations and tried to persuade Chiang to place his armies under American command. Chiang made a pretence of agreeing with Roosevelt's suggestion, but as he did nothing to implement it the futility of Stilwell's position gradually became apparent.

Unfortunately for Stilwell, his recommendations bore the implication that what China needed was Mao Tse-tung rather than Chiang Kai-shek: virtually all observers had remarked upon the honesty, dedication, and efficiency of the Communist commanders. Such reasoning did not fit in with American preconceptions, formed by wartime propaganda about the courageous allies the United States had in Generalissimo and Madame Chiang Kai-shek. Patrick Hurley, who was sent out by Roosevelt in September 1944, took a different position. Hurley's mission was to get the Nationalists, with American support, to prosecute the war against Japan. When Ambassador Gausse resigned on 1 November to protest Stilwell's recall, Hurley succeeded him as US Ambassador to China. Ambassador Hurley was soon won over to the idea, which was sedulously urged upon him by the Chiangs, that the Communists were China's major problem and that only when they had been dealt with could China deal with Japan.

Ambassador Hurley took an active part in negotiations between Chungking and Yenan, which began in November 1944 and continued until February 1945. They broke down over a fundamental divergence of views which was still unresolved at the time of the Marshall Mission to China a year later. According to the Kuomintang, the military integration of Communist forces into the National Army was a precondition for any broadening of the government which would give the Communists real influence over its functioning. In the Communist view, the ending of the one-party dictatorship of the Kuomintang in the National government and the creation of a 'coalition government' must precede surrender by the Communists of exclusive control over their military forces. Chiang wanted military unification first; Mao demanded coalition government first. In the role of mediator Hurley created the impression, both in Chungking and in Yenan, that the United States really intended to back the Nationalists in their determination to force the Communists to capitulate. This impression was strengthened by Hurley's refusal to allow any direct US military aid to the Communists for use against Japanese and puppet troops and his expressed conviction that all such aid be placed under the exclusive control of the Nationalist government. As Stilwell had learned, Chungking would not employ US military aid in fighting the Japanese but would hoard it for eventual use against the Communists.

When Japan surrendered on 15 August, the Communist forces which were in control of the surrounding countryside sought to enter the cities of north China and to disarm the Japanese troops garrisoned there. They were forestalled by an order issued from Tokyo by General MacArthur, the ranking Allied commander in the Far East, in which the Japanese in China proper were instructed to surrender only to Chinese Nationalist forces. The principal cities of north China were occupied by US marines pending the arrival of Nationalist troops, which had to be brought from south and west China. Between 400,000 and 500,000 Nationalist troops were transported to north China in US planes and ships, thereby enabling them to effect the surrender of the Japanese garrison. As fighting between Communist and Nationalist troops became widespread, the headquarters of the US military mission, now installed in Shanghai, camouflaged the American role in the conflict as being concerned solely with the evacuation of Japanese forces from China. When General Marshall arrived in December 1945 to mediate the conflict, he soon recognized that the US could not be impartial in a dispute in which it was actively supporting one side against the other. The Marshall Mission (1945–47), the failure of which was virtually a foregone conclusion, only further embittered the Chinese Communists, while the US military assistance which continued to flow to the Nationalists could not prevent their ultimate collapse. It finally became apparent that only the commitment of US forces on a large scale could prevent a Communist victory. This alternative was rejected by Washington.

Inflation

The history of the Nationalist movement from 1924 to 1949 is the record of a Party which constantly became more dictatorial and self-seeking as it lost the support, one after the other, of all the interested groups whose backing was essential to its survival. In 1927–28 the Kuomintang turned on the peasants and workers who had done so much to make possible its victory in the Northern Expedition. The adherence of the bourgeoisie partially compensated for this loss. However, private enterprise did not flourish in Nationalist China, where official nepotism favoured the growth of 'bureaucrat capitalism'. During the 1930s Nanking's rule rested mainly upon its alliance with foreign interests and regional warlords. Chiang Kai-shek thus turned his regime into an obstacle to the main intellectual currents which had been coursing through China since the May Fourth movement: opposition to imperialism and opposition to warlordism. China's modern intellectuals were further alienated by the Confucian revival proclaimed in Chiang's New Life Movement.

The Japanese occupation checked, and to some extent reversed, the Kuomintang's loss of popular support, but in unoccupied China the deteriorating position of the Nationalists was marked by their increasing use of police terror. At the war's end the main cities of China welcomed the returning Nationalists as liberators from the Japanese yoke, but the bourgeoisie soon regretted the departure of the Japanese as the 'Chungking people' turned out to be carpet-baggers rather than liberators. Meanwhile, the big landlords who had returned with Chiang's armies were discovering that only a successful conclusion of the civil war would make it possible for them to reclaim their former positions in the north China countryside. Student demonstrations protesting the government's failure to avert economic chaos and civil war, held throughout the country in May and June 1947, manifested the disillusionment that was becoming widespread. In the following year Chiang felt obliged to ban the Democratic League, a liberal party of the bourgeoisie. By the time the Kuomintang was driven from the mainland in 1949 it had lost all popular support and become merely a group of profiteers protected by a small but faithful military organization. To a large extent, therefore, the Kuomintang had destroyed itself before its final disaster at the hands of the People's Liberation Army.

One of the principal means by which it achieved its own destruction was inflation. Prices in China rose as much during 1945–48 as they had during eight years of war, and this was not yet the end of an inflationary spiral which destroyed the middle class, the group which provided the main support for liberal government. At the end of the war, average prices were 2,500 times the pre-war level; by late summer 1948, prices had risen to a level 2,500 times that of August 1945. For the whole period 1937–48, then, prices multiplied more than six million times. To achieve such a phenomenal rate of inflation, government printing presses had to be kept going full speed; the face value of bank notes eventually fell below the cost of printing them. In 1948 the government instituted a currency 'reform' with the issue of the 'gold *yuan*'. One new dollar, said to be backed by impressive reserves, was exchanged for three million of the old, but this measure only led to further ruin and cynicism since the government continued to finance approximately two-thirds of total expenditures by monetary expansion. 'Gold *yuan*' notes were soon cascading from the printing presses. The workers were spared to some extent because in many factories wages were pegged to prices, but the salaries of professional people were less elastic. The monthly salary of a teacher or government servant was often only enough to maintain a family for a few days. Savings were wiped out. China's economic situation became one of havoc, with inflation reinforcing the dislocation inevitably resulting from civil war. Unemployment in the cities rose as raw materials became unobtainable and markets shrank, yet a constant stream of refugees descended upon the cities from the countryside. The country's gold reserves, which had stood at an all-time high at the end of the war, were soon dissipated; they fell by 50 per cent during 1946 alone.

At the time of the Japanese surrender, China's economic prospects were extremely good. Industrial expansion in Taiwan and Manchuria under the Japanese had been such that the uniting of these areas with China proper would have increased by several times the country's overall industrial output. Industry had expanded in the former treaty ports, too, and was now in a healthier state then ever before. Moreover, industrial expansion under the Japanese gave China an enviable economic balance, with heavy industries predominating in Manchuria, agricultural production and processing in Taiwan, and light industries in the coastal cities of China proper. These industries, regarded by the Kuomintang as enemy property, were seized at the end of the war and farmed out to Party stalwarts who reaped quick profits at the expense of the economy as a whole. Factories which were not immediately profitable were frequently scrapped, while established businessmen often found it impossible to obtain the import and other licences controlled by the Kuomintang. The dismantling and removal of industrial machinery in Manchuria by the Russians, who had laid claim to it at Yalta as war booty, did not seem particularly reprehensible by comparison with the rapacity of the Nationalists there. In Taiwan, carpet-bagging on the part of the Nationalists was so unrestrained as to cause open revolt in 1947. It was brutally suppressed by the Nationalist army, which, naturally, attributed the unrest to Communist agitation.

This systematic looting of the country by the Nationalists explains why business, professional, and academic people were not greatly alarmed by the prospect of Communist rule. For them, the present was worse than any conceivable future. The wrath of the urban middle class was frequently vented against the United States, accomplice to the crimes of the Nationalists, since this was less dangerous than open criticism of Kuomintang members. Thus, during 1947 there were enormous public protests in north China against the reported raping of Chinese coeds by US marines and the alleged re-arming of Japan by the US occupation authorities. Meanwhile, thanks to US aid, the civil war continued, causing millions of casualties. On a visit to the United States, aging warlord Feng Yü-hsiang lashed out at US aid to the Nationalists, comparing it with the infamous Japanese loans to the Tuan Ch'i-jui clique 30 years earlier.

Civil war

Mao Tse-tung did not attend the Sixth Congress of the CCP, held in 1928. That congress was held in Moscow, in part because it was too dangerous to hold it in China and in part because the critical condition of the Central Committee made it unusually dependent on Moscow. How different was the atmosphere of the CCP's Seventh Congress! Convening at Yenan in April 1945, delegates from the newly-liberated areas joined those from the local Shensi–Kansu–Ninghsia base region to plan for the victory which was now almost in sight. Russian influence was distinguished by its absence. In the case of China, at least, the 1943 abolition of the Comintern had been more than an empty gesture. 'Two roads lie before the Chinese people', Mao said in his opening speech to the Congress. 'Either a China which is independent, free, democratic, united, prosperous and strong . . ., a new China whose people have won liberation, or a China which is semi-colonial, semi-feudal, divided, poor and weak, that is, the old China.'

At the end of the Second World War Yenan controlled a regular army of a million men and 16 liberated areas with a combined population of 100,000,000, a fourth of the total. The Nationalist army facing the People's Liberation Army (PLA) numbered 3,700,000, and it was much better armed. Yet within 18 months of the beginning of full-scale civil war in July 1946, following the failure of Marshall's attempted mediation, the PLA had achieved parity with the Nationalist army. This made it possible for the PLA, which had always held the initiative at the tactical level, to take the strategic offensive and, in a series of decisive engagements, to eliminate the Nationalist armies from the battlefield. The Communists emerged victorious despite the fact that they received far less aid from the Russians than the Nationalists did from the Americans. In the post-war years the United States provided the Nationalists with $1 billion in military hardware and another $1 billion in economic assistance, while the Russians did nothing for the Chinese Communists apart from allowing stocks of weapons surrendered by the Japanese in Manchuria to fall into their hands. After only slight use, much of the US equipment given to the Nationalists was inherited by the PLA, as well.

In north China the military situation quickly reached a stalemate following the Second World War. The Nationalists, supported by Japanese, puppet, and American forces, had taken over the cities, while the Communists retained their hold on the countryside. During 1946 and 1947 the real contest was over control of Manchuria. Traversing Inner Mongolia, PLA forces under Lin Piao had gained control of the Manchurian countryside during the latter part of 1945 and would have prevented the Nationalists from seizing the key cities of Manchuria had not the Russians, responding to a plea from Chiang Kai-shek, delayed their scheduled departure by six months. This made it possible for the Nationalists, with increasing US military assistance, to break through the pass to Manchuria at Shanhaikuan and to capture Mukden and Changchun. In doing so, however, Chiang fatally overextended his armies. General Wedemeyer, the senior US military figure in China, had advised Chiang in late 1945 not to attempt the conquest of Manchuria but to consolidate his position in the south; Wedemeyer did not think the Nationalists could maintain themselves even in north China without arriving at a political compromise with the Communists. The Communists, in contrast, had evacuated their units from south China, including the Yangtze valley, in order to concentrate their forces in the north. As in north China, the Nationalist troops in Manchuria took up positions within city walls or isolated themselves in forts and blockhouses strung out along the main railways.

During 1947 the tide of battle turned against the Nationalists. In the fighting of 1948 the Communists gradually restricted their enemy to fewer and fewer urban strong-points; by January 1949 the Nationalists could no longer even attempt a coordinated defence. The Manchurian phase of the struggle reached its climax in the Liaoning campaign of October 1948 when 400,000 Nationalist soldiers were killed, wounded, or captured by the army of Lin Piao. The fate of north China was decided in the battles of Kaifeng (May 1948), Tsinan (September 1948), and Hsuchow (November 1948– January 1949). In these battles the disciplined and magnificently-led Communist forces were aided by defections from the ranks of the enemy and by poor coordination among the various Nationalist armies, which were often left to fend for themselves. Tientsin and Peking were peacefully liberated in January 1949, thanks in part to the reputation the PLA had gained for itself as an army which, unlike its adversary, did not indulge in rape and pillage.

While the PLA paused at the Yangtze River, negotiations were held between the two sides from February to April 1949. Li Tsung-jen, a leader of the Kwangsi clique who had frequently been at odds with Chiang Kai-shek, had been elected Vice-President of the National government in May 1948. President Chiang correctly inter-preted this as a personal defeat, and in January 1949 he turned the government over to Li. While Chiang prepared for his withdrawal to Taiwan, Acting President Li sought by means of negotiation to spare south China from civil war. But Chiang had retained real power in his own hands, while, on the Communist side, Mao Tse-tung's terms amounted to a demand for unconditional surrender. The talks came to nothing, and on 20 April 1949 the PLA crossed the Yangtze.

On the same day, the British frigate HMS *Amethyst* was fired upon and disabled in the Yangtze by the Chinese Communists, who charged that the ship was violating Chinese waters. The Chinese public was delighted. It was the end of an era. No longer would China tolerate the insult of having foreign ships sail at will on its internal waterways.

By the time the PLA crossed the Yangtze, Chiang had already withdrawn 300,000 troops to Taiwan. Little real fighting occurred in the capture of south China as one commander after another went over to the Communists or fled. After taking Nanking in April and Shanghai in May, the PLA reached Canton, Swatow, and Amoy in October, and the west China cities of Kweiyang, Chungking, and Kunming in November and December. Meanwhile the far northwest fell into the lap of the Communists following the capture of Lanchow at the end of August. Only Hainan, Tibet, and Taiwan still remained beyond the CCP's grasp when the People's Republic of China was formally established in Peking on 1 October 1949.

CHAPTER FIVE

Consolidation of the New Regime

Character of the regime

Just as the decline of imperial China in the nineteenth century coincided with the ascendancy of Western maritime empires, so the appearance of Communist China in the twentieth century coincided with the era of the cold war. It was evident to Mao Tse-tung that US involvement in the Chinese civil war sprang from the same anti-Communism which underlay its post-war policies in Europe. In saluting the establishment of the Cominform, the new organization for Soviet-satellite coordination set up in 1947, Mao had denounced the Marshall Plan as an American plot to dominate Europe. It appeared to the Chinese Communists, as to the Russians, that the US had taken upon itself the anti-Communist mission of the defeated Axis powers. In Eastern Asia, the United States took up the positions vacated by the Japanese. Coming to power within this particular international context, the Chinese Communists sought to harmonize their policies with those of Moscow. Stalinist tenets enjoyed an unparalleled influence on both the domestic and foreign policies of the CCP during the early years of the regime. Not until the Communist Party of the Soviet Union (CPSU) abandoned Stalin's tough anti-American stand in 1956 did Maoist tenets once again monopolize the ideological field in China.

Between 1949 and 1954 the People's Republic of China (PRC) became firmly rooted, both politically and economically, in China and won wide international acceptance. There followed, from 1955 to 1957, a period of rapid change known as 'socialist transformation'. With the inauguration of the Great Leap Forward and commune movements in 1958, Communist China broke out of the limitations imposed by the Soviet development model and began a phase of experimentation. These advances were consolidated during the years 1962–65, which saw the PRC veer sharply away from the Soviet Union in foreign as well as domestic policy.

The period of consolidation is bounded by the promulgation of the Common Programme of 1949 and the Constitution of 1954. The Common Programme had the force of a provisional constitution. It was adopted by the Chinese People's Political Consultative Conference (CPPCC) at its first session, held at the end of September in Peking, the newly designated capital. The CPPCC consisted of over 500 delegates, selected to represent the politically significant sectors of national opinion. Non-Communist intellectuals, religious personages, and members of minor political parties, as well as workers' and peasants' delegates, participated. The composition of the CPPCC reflected the united front, a CCP device which was especially prominent during the 'new democratic' phase of the revolution which gave way, in 1953, to the 'transition to socialism'. In that year China's first comprehensive census was taken. At the same time, basic-level representative congresses were chosen by popular ballot. In 1954 people's congresses at the provincial level elected delegates to the National People's Congress (NPC) which met in Peking in September 1954. The first session of the NPC adopted the Constitution of the People's Republic of China. The Constitution was framed in the context of a particular stage of the revolution, that of the transition to socialism. Although this stage has now been superseded, the 1954 Constitution has remained as the basic state document.

In both the Common Programme and the Constitution the PRC is described as a 'people's democratic dictatorship'. Mao defined this concept in his essay 'On the People's Democratic Dictatorship', written a few months before the establishment of the new regime on 1 October 1949. Included among 'the people' were the petty bourgeoisie and the national bourgeoisie (that is, entrepreneurs with small and medium-sized enterprises) in addition to the working class and the peasantry. The Party represented these four classes, and not the proletariat alone as in the Soviet Union. On the national flag these four classes are represented by four stars grouped around a larger star representing the Party. Excluded from the ranks of the people were the landlord class and the bureaucrat-capitalist class, made up of the biggest entrepreneurs. The people, the beneficiaries of democracy, were to exercise a dictatorship over the latter groups, described as representatives of feudalism and imperialism. This meant a reversal of the class relationships existing during the warlord and Nationalist eras.

Externally, the PRC aligned itself with the Soviet Union and the socialist camp in opposition to 'imperialism'. It 'leaned to one side'. 'Sitting on the fence will not do', Mao said in the same essay. 'Nor is there a third road.' Mao looked upon the Soviet Union as a development model and military ally. In the era of nuclear weapons and the cold war, it could safeguard the fledgling Chinese Communist state whose revolutionary path was menaced by the United States, the most powerful country in the world. Of no less importance was the Soviet Union as an ideological ally. Communism had come to China by way of the Soviet Union; the October Revolution was the forerunner of the Chinese revolution. Marxism–Leninism provided the system of thought which in China superseded Confucianism, and Marxism–Leninism could not be conceived of apart from the Soviet Union. Thus, Chinese membership in the Soviet camp was essential to the political legitimacy claimed by the new leadership in Peking: the Sino-Soviet alliance was referred to specifically both in the Common Programme and in the Constitution.

As in the Soviet Union, the structure of the state in China is distinct from the organization of the Party. The government implements policies developed by the Party in the name of the people. The will of the people is manifested in the people's congresses at each level of administration: national, provincial, county, and township. According to the Common Programme and the Constitution, these people's congresses supervise the functioning of the people's councils, or administrative bodies, at each level. But there is also an organ of the CCP at each level, and it is really the Party which supervises the functioning of the government; the Party also supervises the election of representatives for the people's congresses. These congresses endorse policies already decided upon by the Party and then pass them on to the people's councils for implementation, carried out, once again, under the watchful eye of the Party. Thus, there is a triangular relationship among Party, state, and people. The people participate, the Party directs, and the government implements.

The organization of the CCP is set forth in the Party constitutions of 1945 and 1956, enacted by the Seventh and Eighth National Party Congresses. Democratic centralism and the commitment to establish socialism and communism in China are the guiding principles of the

The Nucleus of Leadership, 1960

Note: ordinary (non-italic) type signifies membership of
Central Committee, capitals indicating Politburo membership

MILITARY	PARTY	GOVERNMENT
National Defence Council and Ministry of Nat. Def.	*Politburo members and alternate members*	*PRC, State Council and Commissions*
LIU SHAO-CH'I	MAO TSE-TUNG	LIU SHAO-CH'I
P'ENG TEH-HUAI	LIU SHAO-CH'I	CHOU EN-LAI
LIN PIAO	CHOU EN-LAI	CH'EN YÜN
LIU PO-CH'ENG	CHU TEH	LIN PIAO
HO LUNG	CH'EN YÜN	TENG HSIAO-P'ING
CH'EN YI	LIN PIAO	TUNG PI-WU
TENG HSIAO-P'ING	TENG HSIAO-P'ING	CH'EN YI
LO JUNG-HUAN	LIN PO-CH'Ü	LI FU-CH'UN
Lo Jui-ch'ing	TUNG PI-WU	PENG TEH-HUAI
Hsü Hsiang-ch'ien	P'ENG CHEN	HO LUNG
Nieh Jung-chen	LO JUNG-HUAN	LI HSIEN-NIEN
Yeh Chien-ying	CH'EN YI	T'AN CHEN-LIN
T'an Cheng	LI FU CH'UN	ULANFU
Hsiao Ching-kuan	P'ENG TEH-HUAI	LU TING-YI
Su Yü	LIU PO-CH'ENG	PO I-PO
Ch'en Keng	HO LUNG	Lo Jui-ch'ing
Wang Shu-sheng	LI HSIEN-NIEN	Nieh Jung-chen
Hsü Kuang-ta	K'O CH'ING-SHIH	Liao Ch'eng-chih
Hsü Shih-yu	LI CHING-CH'ÜAN	Teng Tzu-hui
Liu Ya-lou	T'AN CHEN-LIN	Hsi Chung-hsün
Liao Han-sheng	ULANFU	*Soong Ch'ing-ling*
Ch'eng Ch'ien	CHANG WEN-T'IEN	
Chang Chih-chung	LU TING-YI	
Fu Tso-yi	CH'EN PO-TA	
Wei Li-huang	K'ANG SHENG	
	PO I-PO	

CCP. The Central Committee elected by each national congress, and
more particularly the Political Bureau (Politburo) chosen by the
Central Committee, is the real guiding hand in all Chinese Communist
affairs. Key government personnel are Party members, the most important state positions being held by Central Committee members.

Thus, supervision of the government by the Party is reinforced by interlocking membership. The principal links between the CCP and the people are local Party committees, mass organizations, and institutions of the united front. Every social unit has its Party nucleus. These may be locational units, such as village or street, or vocational units, such as school, factory, production brigade. Peasant associations, labour unions, women's organizations, and student unions are the most important mass organizations supervised by the CCP, while religious organizations, writers' unions, and 'democratic' parties are among the institutions of the united front. The purpose of the united front is to organize that part of the population which is distinct from the masses as well as from the CCP—in other words, the non-Communist intelligentsia. The CCP is everywhere supplemented by the Young Communist League (YCL), known before 1956 as the New Democratic Youth League.

The state structure of China is outlined in the Common Programme, supplemented by the 'Organic Law of the Central People's Government' and the Constitution. Administration is the responsibility of the State Council (called the Government Affairs Council before 1954), headed by a premier, and its subordinate ministries and commissions. A system of people's courts and procuratorates administers justice. Military affairs are the responsibility of the National Defence Council (before 1954, the Revolutionary Military Council). But the Common Programme and the Constitution go beyond the mere description of the state structure of China: they also reflect the programme of the Party. Being programmatic as well as descriptive, they are therefore subject to modification by other declarations of public policy, such as the First Five-Year Plan (1955). All such state documents, in turn, are further modified by the communiqués of the Central Committee and the reports of its Chairman, Mao Tse-tung. Change, not stability, is the outstanding feature of the People's Republic of China.

Consolidation

On the eve of its capture of Peking in January 1949, the CCP was still a peasant-military movement based on the north China countryside. It now faced the tasks of extending its authority to urban areas and carrying the revolution into south China. Meeting in March, the Central Committee adopted a resolution calling for a shift in emphasis of Party work from the countryside to the cities. In the south, the

PLA seized the cities first and then extended its authority into the surrounding rural areas. This was the reverse of the pattern of guerrilla warfare which had characterized PLA operations in the north. The base areas once held by the Communists in the south had been virtually eliminated by the time of the Long March. In the major cities, similarly, the CCP had lost the influence it had exercised among the workers prior to Chiang Kai-shek's counterrevolution of 1927. It took the Party three years to re-establish itself in the cities throughout the country and in the rural areas of south China. By 1953 the whole country was ready to go ahead with the First Five-Year Plan.

The chaos which had facilitated the Communist takeover was the first challenge to the new regime. Agricultural and industrial production had to be restored as quickly as possible. The food situation in the cities, aggravated by the Nationalist blockade of much of the coast, was critical; inflation and urban unemployment were more serious than ever; farming in the grain-surplus provinces south of the Yangtze had been disrupted in the final year of civil war. To meet this situation the Communists adopted a lenient policy toward urban and rural capital, contenting themselves for the time being with the elimination of persons classed as traitors and counterrevolutionaries. Many people who would have fallen into this category had already fled to Taiwan. For those who remained, a reign of terror commenced with the inauguration of the new regime, which initially took the form of a military occupation. Many 'enemies of the people' were summarily executed.

If Manchuria is included, three-quarters of China's industrial capital was in the hands of foreigners in 1945. The Japanese share, comprising the major part of it, was taken over by the Kuomintang and turned into 'bureaucrat capital'. The enterprises in this category were the largest and most modern in China. Seized outright by the Communists, they were made the foundation of the wholly state-owned sector of the Chinese Communist economy. British firms accounted for most of the 15 per cent of non-Japanese foreign industrial capital existing in China in 1945. Before allowing them to withdraw in 1952, the Communists succeeded in draining away a good deal of the capital reserves from their London offices. When the British and other foreign capitalists retired from the scene, their enterprises were added to the state-owned sector.

Legitimate Chinese capitalists, on the other hand, were encouraged to stay in business. They comprised the 'national bourgeoisie' and the 'petty bourgeoisie'. The Communists permitted them to make high profits, but in 1952 much of this was taken back, in the form of fines, during the Five-Anti campaign (against bribery, tax evasion, fraud, theft of government property, and theft of state economic secrets). At the height of the campaign, in January and February, the suicide rate among Chinese capitalists in Shanghai reached 100 per day. Nearly half a million private enterprises were investigated. In the wake of the Five-Anti campaign the government instituted joint public-private management over the medium-sized enterprises of the national bourgeoisie. Control of the small establishments of the petty bourgeoisie was achieved by means of the government's regulation of wholesale and retail trade. With commerce and banking under its control, the government stopped the inflationary spiral which had gripped the country since the outbreak of the Sino-Japanese War. By 1952, price stability had been achieved.

In calling for a shift from a rural to an urban orientation in Party work the March 1949 Central Committee plenum pointed to the need of recruiting more workers into the Party. The number of new members admitted during 1949 and 1950 was as large as the total 1947 membership, and a substantial proportion of these were workers. This trend continued at least until the end of the First Five-Year Plan (1953–57), gradually lessening the preponderance of peasant members which had previously characterized the Party. In 1951 members of peasant origin still comprised 80 per cent of the total, but by 1956 this figure had fallen to 69 per cent. The favouritism shown to workers in the recruitment of Party members is indicative of the privileged position which the industrial proletariat has held generally in Communist China, with its commitment to rapid industrialization.

While the government was establishing its authority in the cities, it was consolidating its hold on the countryside by means of land reform. The Agrarian Reform Law of June 1950 was the fruit of long experience. The radical programme of land redistribution employed by the CCP at the time of the Kiangsi Soviet was politically effective but hurt production. The comparatively moderate programme of land reform used during the Yenan period showed itself to be successful in spurring production in an area already controlled by the Party. In 1946, as the civil war got under way, the radical programme was resumed as the Party sought to expand its area of control. This trend was checked at the end of 1947 by a warning from Mao Tse-tung against ultra-leftism. The Agrarian Reform Law of June 1950 was a compromise. It sought to satisfy the craving of the poor peasants and farm labourers for land without disrupting production. Thus, only the four per cent of the rural population which officially constituted the landlord class were to be expropriated, while the rich peasants were to be allowed to retain all except land rented out to others. The middle peasants were to be protected but their future, like that of the national bourgeoisie, was murky.

Liu Shao-ch'i, Vice-Chairman of the Central Committee, explained that the 1950 Agrarian Reform Law was 'designed to set free the rural production forces from the shackles of the feudal land-ownership system'. It was not anticipated that the equalization of land holdings would bring about an increase in production, but the surplus from existing production would now go to the state rather than to the landlord. The intent of the Law was more political than economic. Land reform would enable the Party to gain a firm hold on the poorer strata of the rural population, providing a sound basis for further social change in the villages. Moreover, land reform was a necessary precondition for agricultural collectivization: eventually the small individual holdings would have to be pooled together, but when this was done the entire rural population would share in the large-scale farms which would result. Increasing the scale of farming was an important way of raising agricultural output, but it was essential that this be done collectively and not privately. In the short run, land reform actually hurt production by increasing the number of individual holdings and by favouring the less efficient producer.

The *hsiang*, or township, was the unit of land redistribution. There are a quarter of a million *hsiang* in China, each with a population of about 1,500. The *hsiang* generally embraces several small hamlets, or natural villages, dominated by one or two clans. For the purposes of land reform, peasant associations were formed by the Party in each *hsiang*. In the first stage, debts were cancelled and rents reduced; then, as the Party compiled data on the local population, accusation meetings were held in which the poorer elements were encouraged to air their grievances; finally, the lands and belongings of those accused of being 'feudal despots' were confiscated. The accused often suffered bodily injury, even death, at the hands of the peasant associations and their auxiliaries, the local militia. Possibly two million landlords were executed during land reform. Countless others were beaten and humiliated. As early as 1927, while organizing the peasants in Hunan, Mao Tse-tung had come to believe that a degree of violence was an indispensable part of effective land reform. Violence, carefully controlled—or contrived—by the Party, could contribute to an effective psychological breakthrough on the part of the majority of the population which stood in judgment of the landlord class.

When a new measure is to be introduced in Communist China, it usually goes through a trial period before being formally enacted. The published order summarizes experience already gained and projects this experience into the future. This was the case with the June 1950 Agrarian Reform Law, which applied to a period of implementation stretching from 1948 through 1952. Generally speaking, north China underwent land reform prior to June 1950, south China after that date. Since the CCP had long been cut off from south China, it had to build an entirely new organization there. The CCP cadres who took charge of land reform in south China were usually northerners unfamiliar with the local dialect. By August 1952, when land reform had been substantially completed in the south, many villages in Manchuria and north China were already organizing mutual-aid teams and cooperatives.

The equalization of land holdings brought to an end two millenia of rural-gentry dominance of the Chinese countryside. The landlords and rich peasants, who had comprised eight per cent of the population and controlled 80 per cent of the land, were proletarianized. This was a political act. In Chinese Communist literature the era of land redistribution is referred to as 'democratic reform'. During 'democratic reform' the economic and political functions of the rural gentry were absorbed by the peasant associations, led by the CCP. By means of the nation-wide elections held in 1953, these peasant associations were transformed into *hsiang* people's congresses. Elections brought to an end the stage of 'democratic reform' and ushered in the stage of 'socialist transformation'. 'Socialist transformation' coincided with the initial stage of the First Five-Year Plan, which was launched in 1953. By the end of 1952, thanks to peaceful conditions and good weather, agricultural production had been fully restored, laying the basis for the further advances expected to result from collectivization.

The Sino-Soviet alliance

Marshal Stalin did not believe that the Chinese Communists could defeat the Nationalists in the civil war. Until the moment that they did, Moscow was pursuing its traditional policy of attempting to control the inner Asian borderlands lying between the two countries. The Sino-Soviet treaty of August 1945 gave the Russians most of what they wanted: Chinese acquiescence in the complete independence of the Mongolian People's Republic (MPR) and in the reestablishment of a Soviet sphere of influence in Manchuria. To determine Soviet rights in China's great north-western region of Sinkiang, where Russians had been extremely active during the 1930s and 1940s, Soviet negotiators continued to meet with Nationalist representatives until the eve of the Communist victory in 1949. Stalin was apparently uncertain as to whether the establishment of the PRC would enhance or prejudice Soviet security. Although he accorded immediate recognition to the new regime, he followed a cautious path in the Sino-Soviet negotiations which ensued.

Mao Tse-tung arrived in Moscow on 16 December 1949 and remained there until 17 February 1950. The discussions which took place during these two months were held in complete secrecy. Three days before Mao's return to Peking, a joint communiqué was issued which revealed the conclusion of three separate agreements. The first was a Sino-Soviet Treaty of Friendship, Alliance, and Mutual Assistance. In committing the two parties to act together in the event of aggression by Japan, or any state collaborating with Japan, the 1950 treaty was in effect an alliance against the United States. The second agreement, in providing for use by the Russians of the Chinese Changchun railroad (embracing both the Chinese Eastern and South Manchurian) and the naval base at Port Arthur, virtually confirmed the Soviet position in Manchuria which had been granted under the 1945 treaty. Soviet financial assistance was the subject of the third agreement: China was to receive credits amounting to US $60 million per year for the five-year period 1950–54 to cover deliveries of industrial and railroad equipment from the Soviet Union. At the same time that Foreign Ministers A. Y. Vyshinsky and Chou En-lai signed these undertakings, they exchanged notes voiding the 1945 treaty and pledging both countries to respect the independence of the MPR.

In the spring of 1950 further agreements were concluded between the USSR and the PRC which provided for the establishment of a Soviet military mission in Peking and the formation of Sino-Soviet joint stock companies. One was to be an airline linking the two countries by three separate routes: via Sinkiang, Mongolia, and Manchuria. Two of the joint stock companies were to operate exclusively in Sinkiang. One was for the exploitation of non-ferrous and rare metals; the other was an oil concession. The fourth company was set up to build and repair ships in Dairen, the Chinese-controlled port in southern Manchuria. In 1954 the Russians agreed to transfer all four joint stock companies to exclusive Chinese control. By this time Moscow had already surrendered all Soviet rights in connection with the Chinese Changchun railroad, and in May 1955 the Soviet garrison force in Port Arthur was replaced by Chinese troops. Not since the nineteenth century had Chinese control of Chinese territory been so complete.

The Chinese and Russians were slow to reach an agreement on Soviet aid for China's First Five-Year Plan. There was still no public announcement of Soviet participation when the Plan commenced in January 1953. Only after Stalin's death in March did it become clear that Soviet aid would be forthcoming. An announcement from Peking in September made it known that the Soviet Union would assist China in the construction or renovation of 141 large-scale enterprises. In October of the following year, on the occasion of the visit to Peking of Khrushchev and Bulganin, the Russians committed themselves to 15 additional major industrial projects. In the spring of 1956, Mikoyan pledged Soviet assistance in connection with 55 more projects, making a grand total of 211.

The industrial equipment supplied to China under these various agreements was covered by short-term credits and repaid by means of Chinese exports to the Soviet Union, mainly of agricultural products, textiles, and minerals. China had completely repaid her debt to the Russians by 1965. China also had to pay for all the technical assistance received from the Soviet Union. Between 1950 and 1960 over 10,000 Russian experts worked in China; during the same period, 8,000 Chinese skilled workers and technicians were given on-the-job training in the Soviet Union. The value of all Soviet participation in China's economic development during the decade amounted to approximately US $2 billion, a sum equivalent to one-tenth the total capital investment under China's First Five-Year Plan. Soviet equipment was of crucial importance to the industrial development of the PRC. If it was priced above comparable Western goods, as has been alleged, the UN-imposed ban on the shipment of strategic goods to China left Peking no alternative. Whereas China's trade with the Soviet Union and Eastern Europe had been negligible before 1949, by 1954 it constituted four-fifths of her total foreign commerce.

If Soviet military aid was more liberal than her economic assistance, it is also true that Chinese arms were to some extent used on Moscow's behalf. This was particularly true in the Korean War, where Chinese intervention rescued Moscow and its North Korean puppet state from a disastrous military situation. China's role in the Indochina War, which enabled the Viet Minh to win a decisive victory over the French, was also beneficial to Moscow. The backing of the Soviet Union, with its nuclear weapons, helped to limit United States involvement in these conflicts and thereby strengthened Peking's hand. But the Sino-Soviet alliance always retained its defensive nature; ultimately, there was the implicit threat of a Soviet invasion of Western Europe should the United States back Chiang Kai-shek in an attempt to invade the Chinese mainland. The alliance has been much too defensive to suit the Chinese, who hoped for stronger Soviet support for Peking's effort to seize Taiwan. Significantly, the Sino-Soviet alliance (February 1950) was concluded prior to the intervention of the US Seventh Fleet in the Taiwan straits (June 1950). Substantial military equipment has been provided for the Chinese under the Sino-Soviet alliance, and this appears to have been given as aid, with no repayment required. During the Korean War, in particular, Chinese units received training from Soviet military experts.

Politically, the Sino-Soviet alliance proved to be as much of a liability as an asset. Moscow's insistence that Peking, rather than Taipei, represent China at the United Nations was of no avail. And when, in January 1950, the Russians boycotted the Security Council to protest the seating of the delegate from Taiwan, it only made possible the passage of the US-sponsored resolution of June 1950 which brought a United Nations force into the Korean War. Peking's tie with Moscow provided grist for the propaganda mills of the Nationalists and their sympathizers throughout the world, who alleged that the Chinese Communists were merely puppets of Moscow. Moreover, Mao's 'lean to one side' policy clashed with the nationalistic and Sino-centric feelings of the Chinese in general, and with a lingering pro-American mystique among the intellectuals and bourgeoisie.

From the formation of the Sino-Soviet alliance in 1950 until Stalin's death two years later a close ideological unity existed between Moscow and Peking. Both were committed to the fulfilment of the sacred task of the world victory of Communism, with the Soviet Union taking the lead in the developed and the Chinese in the underdeveloped countries. Opposed to Communism was imperialism. As CCP Central Committee member Lu Ting-yi put it in 1951: 'The model for revolutions in imperialist countries is the October Revolution; the model for revolutions in colonial and semi-colonial countries is the Chinese revolution.' In practice, this division of responsibility really meant that the Soviet Union was to be paramount in territories overrun by the Germans in the Second World War, while the Chinese sphere was to be the Japanese-occupied territories. This complementarity of interests, framed in the context of a Churchillian world of antagonistic power blocs, crumbled in the mid-1950s as a result of the reassessment of the Soviet position by Stalin's successors.

Korea, Taiwan, Vietnam

Like Germany and Austria in Europe, the Asian states of Korea and Vietnam were left divided by the Second World War. Later, as a result of civil war, China was divided between Taiwan and the mainland. Prior to 25 June 1950, the division of Korea, China, and Vietnam were separate issues, but the North Korean invasion of South Korea on that date, and the swift response of the UN and the US, made them an interconnected cold war problem.

The Korean War was fought in three stages. In the first, beginning on 25 June 1950, troops of the Soviet-oriented Democratic People's Republic of Korea (DPRK) attempted the forcible reunification of the country, left divided at the 38th parallel by the Second World War. Though it overran most of South Korea, the North Korean invasion failed to dislodge American forces from a defensive perimeter around the southern port city of Pusan. The second stage of the war began in October 1950, when forces of the United States and the Republic of Korea (ROK), counterattacking from the south, crossed the 38th parallel in a United Nations bid to reunify the country by force. The UN invasion was checked by Chinese Communist troops which engaged the US and ROK forces on 25 October. By mid-November 300,000 Chinese troops had crossed the Yalu River into North Korea as Chinese People's Volunteers (CPV). On 24 November the UN forces, superior both in numbers and equipment, launched an offensive which General MacArthur said would end the war by Christmas. Instead, by Christmas the CPV had thrown the Americans, South Koreans, and their allies all the way back to the 38th parallel. The third stage of the war was one of strategic stalemate which lasted through the first six months of 1951. Peace talks began in June and spun out for two years. The main stumbling block was the refusal of CPV and DPRK prisoners of war to return home, the UN insisting on voluntary, and the Communist side on mandatory, repatriation.

The People's Republic of China was not directly involved in the first stage of the Korean War. At the outset, Moscow and Pyongyang appear to have been confident of swift victory. Only when the tide of battle turned did the PRC begin the precautionary movement of troops into Manchuria. That point in the war had already been reached by mid-August when the United States intimated, through its representative at the United Nations, that it would press for the military reunification of Korea. Chou En-lai responded to this threat with a declaration of China's interest in the Korean question. During the first few days of October warnings were transmitted to Washington and Lake Success that China would intervene if US troops attempted to conquer North Korea. Peking might have tolerated the breech of the 38th parallel if a rump North Korean state could have been preserved as a buffer; it might even have tolerated the overthrow of the DPRK by a purely South Korean effort. But the overthrow of that regime by United States forces, which would pose a direct threat to Manchuria, could not be accepted.

The spectacular success of the Chinese military intervention greatly enhanced Peking's prestige both at home and abroad. It demonstrated the will and ability of the new regime to defend Chinese national interests, even against the United States. Internally, the 'Resist America, Aid Korea' movement was one of the most important mass campaigns carried out during the early years of the PRC. China's participation in the war, while costly, was also of benefit to her armed forces. The PLA was re-equipped and retrained by the Soviet Union, which also provided China with a jet air force superior to that of any other Asian country. But the intervention of the PRC wrecked whatever chance it might have had of being seated in the UN. In the spring of 1951 the General Assembly passed a resolution branding the PRC an 'aggressor' in Korea. However, Peking's interest in the representation issue had been diminished by Washington's demonstrated ability to bend the UN to its own purposes.

The Korean War also spoiled Peking's chance of seizing Taiwan and thus terminating the Chinese civil war. During the spring of 1950 the Chinese Communists had developed their capability for amphibious operations as they seized a number of small off-shore islands which the Nationalists had been using to blockade Chinese ports; in

April they took the large island of Hainan in the South China Sea. By June they were prepared for the invasion of Taiwan, recognized by all interested parties as an integral part of China. The United States had already indicated that it would not defend the island against a Chinese Communist invasion. This situation was completely transformed by the DPRK crossing of the 38th parallel on 25 June. In ordering US support for the ROK resistance in Korea on 27 June, President Truman also ordered the neutralization of the Taiwan Straits by elements of the US Seventh Fleet. The UN Security Council resolution of the 25th, condemning the North Korean invasion, had made no mention of Taiwan. Thus, the United States had unilaterally brought Taiwan within its defensive perimeter in the Western Pacific. Foreign Minister Chou En-lai immediately denounced the US move as 'armed aggression against the territory of China in total violation of the United Nations Charter'. Chou renewed the PRC's pledge to liberate Taiwan regardless of US interference, but it soon became apparent that the planned invasion had been indefinitely postponed.

The position of the US was anomalous. Like Taipei and Peking, Washington insisted that there was one China, not two. If this were so then the US was clearly involving itself in the Chinese civil war, although Washington tried to avoid this implication by presenting the problem in the context of the cold war. Like the United States, a majority of United Nations members continued to recognize the émigré 'Republic of China' on Taiwan as the government of all China. Britain continued to recognize the PRC, but Peking resented the elaborate 'consulate' which London maintained on Taiwan. Recognition of the PRC implied support of Peking's claim to China's seat in the UN and the ejection of the Republic of China delegate. The Soviet Union, India, and other states which sympathized with Peking's position repeatedly brought the representation and Taiwan questions up in the United Nations, but these moves never achieved any clear result. Washington might have reconsidered its position following the cessation of hostilities in Korea had it not been for the fact that by that time it had become deeply involved in the Indochina War. Finally, in December 1954, the United States concluded a mutual defence treaty with the Republic of China. This move further stimulated the clamour for self-determination on the island, where nine million Taiwanese were misgoverned by the two million Nationalists who had fled from the mainland.

Whereas Soviet troops had carried out the liberation of North Korea from the Japanese, Indochina north of the 16th parallel was liberated by Chinese troops. Both central government troops and provincial troops of Lung Yün, Governor of Yunnan, took part. Like other areas liberated by the Nationalists, North Vietnam was ravaged by these armies. Anything of value which could be moved disappeared; what was not seized as war booty by the higher-ups was carried off by the soldiers, from whom no woman was safe. During 1946 the Chinese were replaced by the French, who had already been reintroduced into southern Indochina by the British occupation authorities. Their return to the north was agreed upon by Ho Chi Minh, probably under pressure from the Russians, who were then more concerned about the prospects of Communism in France than in French Indochina. Ho's dilemma derived from the fact that he was both a veteran Communist and Vietnam's outstanding nationalist. By December his Viet Minh forces were at war with the French.

During the winter of 1949–50 the Chinese Communists reached the North Vietnamese frontier and began giving military aid to the Viet Minh. United States military aid began flowing to French forces after the outbreak of the Korean War in 1950. By the time the decisive battle of Dien Bien Phu commenced in early 1954, the United States was paying 80 per cent of total French army expenditures in the Indochina War. Nevertheless, the reinforced French garrison at Dien Bien Phu succumbed to the Viet Minh, who now had Chinese artillery, on 7 May, and the war was terminated at Geneva on 20 July 1954.

The Geneva Conference on Indochina implicitly recognized the great-power status of the People's Republic of China. A key role at the conference was played by Premier Chou En-lai, despite the fact that the American Secretary of State, John Foster Dulles, refused to shake hands with him. The British Foreign Secretary, Sir Anthony Eden, was more diplomatic, and the successful conclusion of the conference was due in large part to his efforts. Soviet Foreign Minister V. M. Molotov remained in the background, thereby according his Chinese colleague the status in South-east Asian matters which Peking considered its due. Both Chou En-lai and the French Premier, Pierre Mendès-France, were pleased with the Geneva settlement, which left Vietnam divided at the 17th parallel. The French had succeeded in extricating themselves from a hopeless military situation without too much loss of face; China had regained its traditional sphere of influence in the Red River valley, now ruled by the Democratic Republic of Vietnam.

Thus, by the summer of 1954 the cold-war front in the Far East had been stabilized. On one side stood China and its client states of North Korea and North Vietnam. On the other side, South Korea, Taiwan, and South Vietnam were the advance positions of the United States, which was deeply entrenched in Japan and Okinawa. Okinawa, the major island in the Ryukyu chain, had become an American preserve following the defeat of Japan; Japan itself was tied into the American defence system by a peace treaty and a security pact signed at San Francisco in 1951 and denounced by the Soviet bloc. South Vietnam was bound by the 1954 Geneva agreement not to join any military alliance, but the South-east Asian Treaty Organization (SEATO) formed in September 1954 provided a means by which this restriction could be circumvented by Washington. South Vietnam was not a member of SEATO, but the protection of the treaty was extended to the Republic of Vietnam which was then taking shape in Saigon.

Centralization

In the PRC, as in other totalitarian states, nothing is private. The state intrudes into every aspect of the nation's life. What had previously been left to the village, the family, and the guild now became the concern of Party and government cadres. Under the empire, the *hsien* magistrate, with responsibility for perhaps a quarter of a million people, had been the lowest official appointed by the state. The gap between the government and the family was filled by the Confucian literati, the class which had a monopoly of wealth as well as learning. What remained of this class after the ravages of the first half of the twentieth century was destroyed by the CCP. The Party then attempted to assume the functions previously performed by the literati. By 1953 it was normal for a *hsiang* (or, in urban areas, a street) to have a CCP branch; in that year Party membership passed the six million mark. Nor was the family any longer autonomous: the Marriage Law of 1950 was an important instrumentality in 'liberating' family relationships. The Marriage Law guaranteed freedom of choice in the selection of husband or wife; legalized divorce; and prohibited 'polygamy, concubinage, child betrothal, interference with the remarriage of widows, and the exaction of money or gifts in connection with marriage'. These practices had previously been widespread. To the extent that the new law could be enforced, it would be one of the most revolutionary factors in the social life of new China. From 1950 to 1953 the regime carried on a vigorous campaign to publicize and enforce the Marriage Law, but it appears to have been more generally adhered to in the cities than in the country.

At the same time, the Party was attempting to dominate the economic life of the country. During 1953 a system of 'planned purchase and supply' of grain and other staples was instituted to enable the state to collect from the peasant what had previously been paid out in rent and interest as well as in taxes. To handle the distribution of commodities, 35,000 state trading companies had been set up by 1953. These were supplemented, at the local level, by supply and marketing cooperatives, which even at that date were being criticized for low efficiency. Through its control of retail and wholesale, as well as foreign, trade, the state was in a position to regulate what manufacturing still remained in private hands. Handicrafts were gradually cooperativized. Moreover, the whole effort at industrialization was a strictly public venture, in the hands of the State Planning Commission established in 1952. The state also undertook a variety of activities which traditionally lay beyond the private sector, such as water conservancy projects. Between 1949 and 1952 over ten million workers were mobilized to dig the equivalent of 23 Suez Canals.

During its first few years the PRC was attempting to carry through simultaneous political, social, and economic revolutions. Politically, it had to digest the government organization left behind by the Kuomintang, which was taken over virtually intact in the newly liberated areas. Socially, it was trying to break up the old clan organization and to infuse the family and village with new values. Economically, it was trying to change the face of China as rapidly as possible without benefit of the profit motive. Directly or indirectly, the main responsibility for this revolutionary effort fell on the Party. As its committees and branches proliferated among the half billion Chinese spread out over a continent-sized country, a country with only the most primitive statistical service and communications system, the Party was soon afflicted by such diseases as 'bureaucracy' and 'complacency'.

A rectification campaign had been carried out in 1950 to raise the ideological and political level of the new recruits—a large proportion of them illiterate—who had swelled the ranks of the Party at the moment of victory. The Three-Anti movement was launched at the

beginning of 1952 to root out the 'waste, corruption, and bureau-
cratism' which had become dangerously widespread among Party
members. During this campaign, which preceded the Five-Anti
campaign aimed at the bourgeoisie, all Party nuclei were reorganized.
The qualifications of each member were reviewed: those found wanting were expelled. Even while the lower echelons of the Party were
being cleansed, a tendency toward personal empire-building was
discovered among senior cadres. In the face of this threat, Liu
Shao-ch'i called for greater Party unity at the February 1954 plenum
of the CCP Central Committee. The 'anti-Party' activities of two
prominent members, Kao Kang and Jao Shu-shih, were revealed at
this time. Kao Kang was accused of trying to set up a separate king-
dom in Manchuria. Following the purge of Kao and Jao, the multi-
province administrative regions were abolished in the latter half of
1954. These greater administrative regions were a legacy of Liberation, which had left China under the authority of six field armies,
each in control of a huge region. Regional bureaux of the CCP
Central Committee had grown up alongside the administrative
regions: these were also abolished in 1954. Under the 1954 Constitution, China was divided administratively into 21 provinces, two
special municipalities, and five autonomous regions, all directly
responsible to the Central People's Government, with the corresponding Party bureaux responsible to the Central Committee. However, there was no guarantee that regionalism would not be succeeded
by provincialism.

The degree of centralization required to rule China as a totalitarian
state placed an enormous—and in the end intolerable—burden on
the Party. The only means at the disposal of the Party and its subordinate organizations in fulfilling their various tasks were propaganda and mass campaigns; its only defences against ossification were
rectification and party purge. The revolutionary ardour which had
fired the Party during its struggle for power and the establishment of
the new regime soon faded. That the PRC was in an impasse was
already suspected by the time the 'transition to socialism' was
officially inaugurated in late 1953.

CHAPTER SIX

The Era of the First Five-year Plan

The First Five-Year Plan

There was general agreement among twentieth-century Chinese
reformers about the need for China to industrialize in order to cope
with domestic social problems and foreign encroachment. What was
novel about the CCP's approach was its reliance on Soviet aid and
experience. Political considerations aside, it was believed that the
Soviet development model provided the best guide to rapid industrialization. A high rate of industrial development would lead fairly
quickly to the high level of industrialization already attained by
leading capitalist states. 'A few decades will be enough', declared
State Planning Commission Chairman Li Fu-ch'un. 'It will take us
only five years to reach or surpass what it had taken decades to
achieve under reactionary rule in China.'

Socialist industrialization of the type instituted by Stalin in the
Soviet Union took heavy industry as the key element. Other sectors
of the economy were to contribute to the rapid expansion of heavy
industry, which would quickly become strong enough to stimulate
general productivity increases throughout the economy. In particular,
consumption was to be severely restricted for the time being, for the
Soviet planners believed that spending and saving were contradictory
and that, unless the people kept their belts tightened for a while, the
capital needed for industrialization could not be accumulated. The
importance of heavy industry for defence purposes was also a
consideration.

China's 'First Five-Year Plan for the Development of the National
Economy' was to run until the end of 1957. It had already been in
operation for two and a half years by the time it was formally pre-

sented to the National People's Congress in July 1955. Up until that time it was carried forward by means of annual plans. Long-range planning was impeded by a variety of factors. Agreement on the scope of Soviet aid was not reached until May 1953, although the Russians had been participating in reconstruction work in Manchuria since 1950. Long-range planning was also made difficult by the lack of data concerning China's existing production and distribution systems. The Communists did not inherit a single, national economy upon which they could impose their development plans. Instead, they found a land of many economies, with a high degree of local, provincial, and regional autarchy. The economy had not only to be expanded, but also to be unified. The heavy-industry complex developed in Manchuria by the Japanese, which was to be the foundation of the First Five-Year Plan, had never been integrated with the economy of the rest of China. Planning with regard to the textile and other consumer-goods industries located chiefly in the coastal cities was complicated by the fact that this sector of the economy was still partly in private hands. Only about half of domestic trade was directly controlled by the state at the end of 1952. While China's international trade had been wholly nationalized, the shift from world markets to barter-type arrangements with the Soviet bloc caused dislocations. The location and extent of the nation's mineral resources was only partially known, and was still being explored. Finally, the demands of the Korean War tended to disrupt normal economic activity.

China's total volume of industrial production was expected to rise 15 per cent annually and to double in the course of the First Five-Year Plan. Of the US $20 billion capital fund for the Plan, 70 per cent was to go into the expansion of the heavy-industry complex, including railroads. Industry in general was to get 58·2 per cent; 88·8 per cent of this amount was to be invested in capital-goods as compared with 11·2 per cent in consumer-goods industries. The agricultural sector was allotted only 7·6 per cent of investment under the Plan, with the remaining 15 per cent going for health, education, and other minor items. Of 694 major projects, the 156 Soviet-aided projects constituted the core of the Plan. The development of these large-scale industries would further enhance the position of the state sector of the economy as compared with the private sector. What remained of capitalist industry and commerce would gradually be taken over by the state, while agriculture and handicrafts would be cooperativized.

The goal of doubling industrial production in the course of the First Five-Year Plan was realized. By maintaining gross domestic investment at the very high level of 19 per cent per year, the Chinese Communists were able to increase industrial output by 120 per cent during the Plan period. As was to be expected, the growth of heavy industry was particularly impressive, with steel and chemical fertilizers showing a four-fold increase and coal and cement output more than doubling. Electric power and petroleum production increased nearly three times. The tonnage of freight hauled on China's railroads doubled between 1953 and 1957, while over 5,000 miles of new lines were added to the rail network. However, many of the targets for consumer goods production were not attained, and in 1954 nationwide rationing of cotton cloth had to be introduced in order to counter inflationary pressures. During the period of the First Five-Year Plan school enrolment more than doubled, while health facilities were greatly expanded.

The rapid expansion of the capital-goods sector of the economy continued into the period of the Second Five-Year Plan (1958–62). In general terms, about half of the basic industrial development envisioned by the architects of the First Five-Year Plan was to be achieved during the Second Five-Year Plan. Figures for the following industries are indicative:

	1952	1957 (claim)	1962 (target)
Steel (millions of tons)	1·35	5·35	10·5–12
Cement (millions of tons)	2·9	6·7	12·5–14·5
Electric power output (billions of kilowatts)	7·26	19·03	40 (plus)

Many of the major projects begun during the First Five-Year Plan were only partially completed by 1957. In 1956 Moscow undertook to assist in the construction of 55 large-scale projects in addition to the 156 agreed upon earlier: of these 211 projects, the majority of which were started during the First Five-Year Plan, 68 had been completed by the end of 1957. In 1958, the first year of the Second Five-Year Plan, 45 Soviet-aided projects were completed, and 41 more came into operation by the end of 1960. State capital investment during the first half of the Second Five-Year Plan period approximated the total investment for the entire period of the First Five-Year Plan, and heavy industry continued to take the lion's share.

A fully elaborated Second Five-Year Plan was never produced: as had been the case prior to 1955, planning was done on an annual basis after 1957 as China went into a new phase of development, that of the Great Leap Forward. The 'First Five-Year Plan for the Development of the National Economy' of 1955 was unique. It reflected the attempt to adapt to Chinese conditions the highly centralized and heavy-industry oriented planning of the Stalinist type. This attempt pre-occupied the People's Republic of China during much of the first decade of its existence. By the time it was abandoned in 1960, the value of China's industrial output had increased four times as compared with 1952: output had doubled between 1953 and 1957 and doubled again from 1958 to 1960. Manufacturing plant capacity rose by at least 15 per cent a year during the period 1952–60 and, though most of this was in heavy industry, the production of consumer goods advanced at the respectable rate of 2–2½ per cent per year. The performance of agriculture, expanding by less than 20 per cent for the entire period of the First Five-Year Plan, was less than expected, yet significant development did occur: the area of land reclaimed during the period 1952–60 approximated the total cultivated area of Britain; at the same time, water conservancy projects greatly extended the area of irrigated land. Although by Western standards China was still a backward and predominantly agricultural country at the end of her experiment with the Soviet development model, her per-capita gross national product was fully a third higher in 1959 than it had been in 1933. During this same period the per capita product in many under-developed countries of the world had actually declined.

The two main faults in the First Five-Year Plan were suspected by many at the time it was published but it was only after several years of experimentation that the leadership became fully cognizant of these inadequacies. The first was the lag of agriculture behind industry. At the beginning of the Soviet Union's First Five-Year Plan (1928–32), there was already an agricultural surplus: the task of the state was simply to collect that surplus without having first, as in China, to create it. The Soviet farmer at that time produced more than twice as much as did the Chinese farmer in the early years of the PRC. Yet, under China's First Five-Year Plan, the agricultural sector had to provide the capital for industrialization, the transfer for this purpose amounting to about 20 per cent of farm output (as compared, for example, with one per cent in India). Agriculture had to provide food for a rapidly growing urban population as well as exports and industrial raw materials. Of the exports with which the government paid for its imports of industrial equipment, 75 per cent came from agriculture, either directly or in processed form; 90 per cent of the raw materials for consumer-goods industries came from agriculture. Part of the burden placed on agriculture by the demands of industrialization was carried by the state farms which absorbed a large share of the investment funds allocated to the agricultural sector under the First Five-Year Plan. The state farms were located mainly on reclaimed land in Sinkiang province in the north-west and in Heilungkiang province in the north-east. In these regions extensive, mechanized agriculture could be practised. Nevertheless, the traditional peasant economy sector was still overburdened. Mao Tse-tung hoped that institutional changes—collectives and communes—would make possible an improvement in the performance of agriculture so that scarce capital would not have to be diverted from the high-priority industrial sector.

The second inadequacy of the First Five-Year Plan was its over-centralization. Centralized planning and decision-making to the extent required by the Plan were not feasible in a country so vast and so poorly endowed with communications and technical personnel as was China. The distance between responsibility and production was too great. After 1957, decentralization did in fact take place.

Socialist transformation

Concurrently with 'socialist construction' under direct state management, the 'socialist transformation' of privately owned agriculture, industry, and commerce was expected to take place during the First and subsequent five-year plans. This is the meaning of the 'transition period' which commenced, along with the First Five-Year Plan, at the beginning of 1953. During this period, the area of state control would gradually be enlarged at the expense of private enterprise, continuing a process already begun during the period of recovery (1949–52). The private sector had been included within the scope of the First Five-Year Plan, which embraced the whole economy and not merely the public sector. Once the private sector was eliminated, the transition to socialism would be complete. Until the middle of 1955 it was thought that 'socialist transformation' would extend over several five-year plans. Then, at the end of July, Mao Tse-tung delivered a report 'On the Question of Agricultural Cooperation', in which he called for a speed-up in the building of cooperative farms.

Mao's report, in which he accused Party cadres of 'tottering along like women with bound feet', prompted a reassessment of the situation by the Central Committee. At a meeting in October 1955 it determined to press forward more rapidly with socialist transformation and resolved that the Eighth National Congress of the CCP should meet in September 1956: by the time it did, private ownership of the means of production had been basically eliminated from Communist China.

In urban areas, the real Chinese capitalists, or 'national bourgeoisie', had not been eliminated during the immediate post-Liberation period, as had the compradore, or 'bureaucrat-capitalist' class. However, they had been brought under such strict government control that they were no longer at liberty to go out of business, even if they desired to do so. Especially after the Five-Anti campaign, their management function was largely restricted to the implementation of state directives. Because of economic pressures, they had little choice but to accept the joint public-private ownership scheme which was the vehicle for their reform. By the time the 'Provisional Regulations Governing Public-Private Jointly Operated Industrial Enterprises' was published in 1954, less than 30 per cent of industrial output remained in private hands. This percentage fell rapidly with the speed-up in socialist transformation in late 1955. Frequently, entire guilds rather than individual factories became joint enterprises. In this sudden campaign, 90 per cent of all industrial concerns which still remained in private hands were converted into joint enterprises. The 'national bourgeoisie' had shed their label, but they continued to function as state employees, and China's need for their skills enabled them to draw good salaries.

Some of the petty bourgeoisie were included, along with the national bourgeoisie, in the joint public-private enterprises; others were brought into cooperatives. As retail trade was taken over by the state, a move which paralleled the nationalization of industry, merchants and peddlers were absorbed into state trading companies and marketing cooperatives. Thus, private commerce was eliminated along with private industry. The ability of the state to regulate prices enabled it to eliminate hoarding and speculation and gave it the means by which resources could be transferred from one sector of the economy to another, as, for instance, between rural and urban areas. At the same time, independent handicraftsmen, both in the towns and the countryside, were cooperativized.

At least two-thirds of the people affected by socialist transformation were engaged in agriculture. They were the small producers who had been favoured, if not created, by land reform (1948–52). Following the autumn harvest of 1955, the cooperative movement was extended to include virtually all of China's 110 million peasant households. In this 'socialist high tide', as Mao referred to it at the end of 1955, China experienced a revolution which was probably more radical than any other instituted by the Communist regime. After cooperativization, it was but a small step to collectivization, basically realized by the end of 1956. In this way the peasant proprietor was proletarianized. Chinese agriculture was less disrupted by this revolution than Soviet agriculture had been. Anxious to avoid the fierce resistance which Soviet collectivization had encountered in the late 1920s and early 1930s, the CCP proceeded cautiously, though rapidly.

The 'socialist transformation' of Chinese agriculture was carried forward by stages: seasonal mutual-aid teams; permanent mutual-aid teams; semi-socialist cooperatives; and, finally, advanced cooperatives, or collectives. As with land reform, the CCP had experimented with various forms of cooperativization during its Soviet (1927–34) and Yenan (1935–45) periods. This experience was applied to Manchuria and north China in the wake of land reform, which began during the civil war. By 1950, as land reform was just beginning south of the Yangtze, 20 per cent of all China's peasant households had already joined together to form mutual-aid teams. By 1953, when the Central Committee issued its 'Decision on Mutual Aid and Cooperation in Agriculture', the figure had risen to 40 per cent. The peak year for mutual-aid teams was 1954, when their number reached ten million, about 40 per cent of which were permanent and the rest seasonal. They were then superseded by agricultural producers' cooperatives (APCs). In December 1951 there were 300 APCs; two years later there were 14,000. In the autumn of 1954 the number of APCs passed 100,000 and in June 1955 it reached 650,000. There then occurred the 'socialist high tide in the Chinese countryside' of which Mao spoke. By the end of 1955 the number of APCs was nearly two million, more than three times the June number. The semi-socialist APCs then gave way to collectives (APCs of the advanced type). 'Model Regulations for Higher Stage Agricultural Producers' Cooperatives' appeared in June 1956. By the end of the year practically all of Chinese agriculture was encompassed by these collectives.

Percentage of house-holds in:	1953	1954	(June) 1955	(Dec.) 1955	1956	1957
Mutual-aid teams	40	60	42			
APCs		11	14	63	8	
Collectives					88	97

A mutual-aid team consisted of an average of seven households which pooled their labour on a seasonal or permanent basis. Draft animals and major items of equipment or fixed capital, which might have accrued to them as a result of the expropriation of landlords, might also be pooled. However, their individual parcels of land remained intact. An APC normally embraced several mutual-aid teams and might have 30 or more households. By merging the family plots of the participants, the APCs made cultivation more efficient. Boundary strips were ploughed up and the entire land-holding of the cooperative farmed as a unit. Frequently, however, the peasants successfully resisted the suggestion that the land taken up by the graves of their ancestors be converted to agricultural use. Income of the members was determined mainly on the basis of their contribution of land and other fixed capital. In the advanced APC, or collective, the main determinant of income was work performed. Whereas the cooperative was essentially a profit-sharing scheme, in the collective the members received wages, the amount of which was determined by the number of work points accumulated during the pay period. With 80 households, the average collective was twice the size of a cooperative and generally corresponded to a hamlet, or natural village.

One of the principal targets of the cooperative movement was the rich peasant, whose continued existence was a reminder that the old order in the Chinese countryside had not been entirely obliterated. As indecision and stagnation overtook the countryside following land reform, the rich peasants had reasserted themselves. Some of the poor peasants could not make ends meet and sold their land; others did well and became 'new' middle peasants, while some middle peasants advanced to the ranks of the rich peasants. The countryside was in danger of again becoming polarized between rich and poor. By means of the cooperatives, which only poor and middle peasants were at first allowed to join, the rich peasants were isolated. When they were eventually allowed to join, they did so on terms set by the cooperative. For all practical purposes, the rich peasant was dispossessed of his capital along with his independence. Economic pressures and propaganda were used against the rich peasant, just as they were against his counterpart in the city, the national bourgeoisie. Moreover, the rising productivity achieved by the cooperatives made joining less onerous than it would have been had output remained stagnant. The golden rule of the APCs was that they must realize higher output.

To carry through the 'socialist high tide' in the Chinese countryside, the CCP had to strengthen its rural organization. Some 700,000 peasants (nearly 10 per cent of total Party membership at that time) were taken into the Party during 1954. This increase in rural membership continued during 1955, spurred on by a national rural-work conference called by the Central Committee in March 1955. By 1956 there were twice as many cadres per capita as there had been in 1952. With the cooperative movement, the social struggle in the villages once again became intense. It was linked to a new campaign against 'counterrevolutionaries'. Under Party leadership, positive elements from among the poor peasants, frequently joined by former PLA men, overturned the old order in the villages. It was believed that rural capitalism in China was being put down once and for all. That there was some dissatisfaction among the rich peasants is suggested by the killing of farm animals which, though limited by comparison with what happened at the time of collectivization in the Soviet Union, was sufficient to prompt a State Council warning on the subject in December 1955. For instance, there were fewer hogs in 1956 than there had been in 1952, but the situation improved in 1957.

The regime was no less determined to increase agricultural production than it was to alter the relations of production in the rural economy. Food-grain production in 1952 had outstripped the record of the best pre-war years and surpassed by nearly 50 per cent the poor year of 1949. The good crop in 1952 no doubt influenced the decision to launch the First Five-Year Plan in 1953. But the poor 1953 harvest, due mainly to unfavourable weather, led to the planned purchase and supply scheme by which the state monopolized the grain market. A black market and a rationing system grew up side by side, while peasants flocked to the cities. Floods made 1954 an even worse year. In September the system of planned purchase and supply was extended to cotton and cotton cloth. By 1955 the agricultural situation had become acute. In August a more drastic system of 'fixed production, fixed purchase, and fixed supply' (the *san-ting*, or three-fix policy) was introduced. New restrictions were imposed on the movement of persons outside their villages. Apart from weather, the poor supply situation was caused partly by an increase in food consumption on the part of the peasants. Whereas per capita food consumption in urban areas declined slightly between 1953 and 1957, the rural population increased its per capita grain consumption by more than 10 per cent. The increase in the acreage sown to industrial crops at the expense of grain also affected food supplies. The bumper 1955 harvest—184 million tons of grain compared to the previous record of 154 million tons in 1952—gave the Party the confidence needed to speed up the cooperative movement and to announce a Twelve-Year Plan for Agriculture (1956–67).

The cooperatives permitted land, labour, and capital to be more rationally combined than had been possible with individual proprietorship. For instance, in the cooperative it was possible for the rural population to find useful employment during the slack season. Whereas the peasant had worked an average of 172 days a year in the 1920s, in 1956 he worked 250 days. This revealed an enormous potential which the Great Leap Forward of 1958–60 would make fuller use of. As the Minister of Agriculture remarked in connection with the Twelve-Year Plan, the fact that five-sixths of the country's 600 million people are peasants is a 'special feature' of China's industrialization. Handicrafts and subsidiary occupations were expected to expand greatly within the framework of the collectives. So vast and remote was rural China in relation to large-scale industry that it was affected but slightly by industrialization. There was little mobility of labour between farm and factory. Perhaps, then, the answer was to bring industry to the farmer.

Eighth Party Congress

The CCP's Eighth National Congress met in Peking from 15 to 27 September 1956. More than a decade had passed since the Seventh Congress in 1945. In that time Party membership had grown from 1·2 to 10·7 million: 90 per cent of all Party members in 1956 had joined since 1945, and 60 per cent had joined since 1949. One of the tasks of the Eighth Congress was to approve a new Party constitution. The most significant difference between the 1945 and the 1956 Party constitutions was that the latter set forth a framework for Party organizations at the level of the rural district, from which sprang a large proportion of the new members. The Eighth Congress also elected a new Central Committee—without, however, disturbing the inherited leadership core of Long March veterans. By this time there were strong indications of the emergence of a 'new-class' mentality within the Party: symptomatic of this trend was a wage increase for bureaucrats.

The views of the Eighth Congress on the economic situation were made known in its 'Proposals for the Second Five-Year Plan' (1958–62). Its prescription was for more of the same. Anticipating the successful conclusion of the First Five-Year Plan in 1957, the Congress envisioned a Second Five-Year Plan which would carry forward the work of the First. It had been recognized as early as the spring of 1956 that the rate of investment in capital-goods industries was too high, leading to disequilibrium among different sectors of the economy as well as to inflationary pressures. Following the industrial 'leap forward' in 1956 by which many of the First Plan targets had been reached, 1957 was envisioned as a year of consolidation and adjustment in the economy preparatory to further growth. The Third Five-Year Plan period was frequently mentioned during the Eighth Congress as the time at which China would have developed all the material prerequisites for socialism. With somewhat more emphasis on agriculture compared with industry, and on light as compared with heavy industry, the economy was expected to expand steadily during the Second and Third Plan periods. As it happened, the Great Leap Forward which commenced in 1958 entirely eclipsed the Second Five-Year Plan, of which little more was heard; the Third Five-Year Plan fell into oblivion. Ch'en Yün, the Politburo member most closely identified with Soviet-style planning, was criticized for being too conservative.

While expressing satisfaction with the rate of growth in the economy, the Eighth Congress criticized in detail both the socialist construction and the socialist transformation which had taken place during the First Five-Year Plan period. Faulty planning had caused considerable waste in industry. For instance, production of a new two-wheeled, double-shared plough ran so far ahead of demand that the nation's steel supply was needlessly depleted. An undue emphasis on the quantitative fulfilment of targets had affected quality: many products, including machine tools, could not be used at all. Shortcomings were also detected in many agricultural producers' cooperatives. Comrades who had pressed forward too hastily with the formation

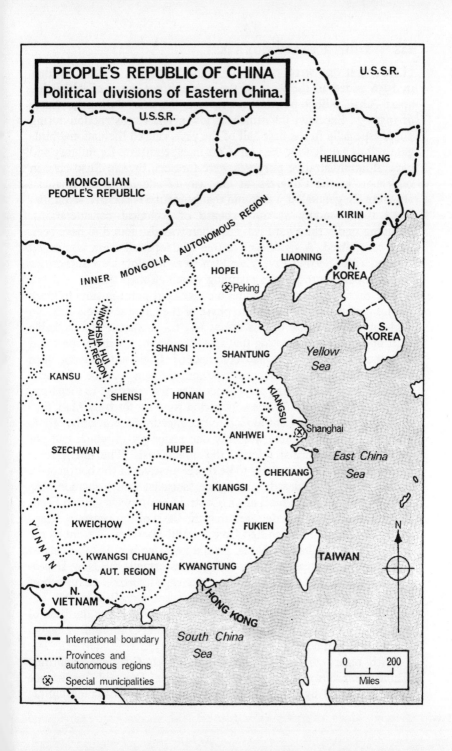

PEOPLE'S REPUBLIC OF CHINA
Political divisions of Eastern China.

U.S.S.R.

U.S.S.R.

HEILUNGCHIANG

MONGOLIAN
PEOPLE'S REPUBLIC

KIRIN

INNER MONGOLIA AUTONOMOUS REGION

LIAONING

HOPEI

N. KOREA

⊗Peking

S. KOREA

NINGHSIA HUI AUT. REGION

SHANSI

SHANTUNG

Yellow
Sea

KANSU

SHENSI

HONAN

KIANGSU

SZECHWAN

HUPEI

ANHWEI

⊗Shanghai

East China
Sea

CHEKIANG

KIANGSI

KWEICHOW

HUNAN

FUKIEN

YUNNAN

KWANGSI CHUANG
AUT. REGION

KWANGTUNG

TAIWAN

N.
VIETNAM

HONG KONG

N

South China
Sea

- -●- - International boundary
- .... Provinces and
  autonomous regions
- ⊗ Special municipalities

0   200
Miles

of cooperatives were guilty of 'blind optimism'. Poor weather in 1956 added to the woes of the cooperatives, some of which fell apart. A half-million peasants migrated to the cities during the winter of 1956–57. Excessive investment in low-priority construction during 1956, especially in the first half of the year, caused the national budget to show a deficit for the year. Cuts in expenditures for military and general administrative purposes were foreseen by Liu Shao-ch'i, in his report to the Congress, as one way of alleviating the financial situation. In general, it was found that bureaucrats had over-administered the economy at the expense of technical considerations. Planning under the First Five-Year Plan was also found to have been over-centralized. A significant degree of decentralization was called for under the Second Five-Year Plan so as to allow local authorities to participate more fully in planning which affected them.

The Eighth Congress provides a convenient point in time to mark the limit of the new-democratic phase of the Chinese revolution. No declaration was made to this effect, but there was an unmistakable shift of emphasis suggesting that new democracy lay in the past and that the era of socialism had commenced. Socialism had not been realized: however, in Communist jargon, the construction of socialism was beginning to take precedence over the transition to socialism, and policy guidelines for the new period were set forth by Mao Tse-tung in a report to a Central Committee meeting in November 1956. In September 1956 there was only one major group which had not yet undergone socialist reform: the intellectuals. The intellectuals were considered by the Party to be representatives of the bourgeoisie, a class which had already undergone 'socialist transformation'. As early as June 1956 the head of the Central Committee's United Front Work Department had declared that the basis of the people's democratic dictatorship had shifted from a multi-class united front to the worker-peasant alliance, that is, from a new-democratic to a socialist basis. As the united front was being transformed, the New Democratic Youth League was preparing to change its name. In his report to the Eighth Congress, Liu Shao-ch'i announced that this 20-million-strong organization, from which the CCP takes the bulk of its new members, would soon become the Young Communist League, a change which actually occurred in May 1957.

With regard to foreign affairs, the Eighth Congress reaffirmed China's commitment to the Five Principles of Peaceful Coexistence first enunciated by Chou En-lai and Nehru in a joint communiqué issued in New Delhi in June 1954. They were: mutual respect for territorial integrity and sovereignty, non-aggression, non-interference in each other's internal affairs, equality and mutual benefit, and peaceful coexistence. These Five Principles had been written into the 1954 Constitution of the PRC and made the basis for the Chinese peace offensive which reached its climax at the Bandung Conference of April 1955. Whatever their misgivings about the Twentieth Soviet Party Congress of February 1956, which criticized Stalin, the Chinese comrades kept to themselves: in September 1956 they spoke only about fraternal aid and solidarity among socialist states. The complementary policies of domestic retrenchment and peaceful coexistence approved by the Eighth Congress were manifestations of conservative influence within the Party, which reached a high-water mark at that time.

The Hundred Flowers

The very success of the First Five-Year Plan raised many new problems. One of the most difficult was that of the role of the technician, who had become the intellectual *par excellence* in the new China. The need for technical personnel increased as industrialization and urbanization made life in China more and more complex. The proliferation of factories, laboratories, and other modern institutions required more and more engineers, scientists, and other professionally-trained people. But the nation's requirement for technical personnel clashed with the determination of CCP cadres to maintain their monopoly of authority. The technicians considered themselves intellectuals—as in traditional China, a class apart from the less educated. The cadres, who tended to think that their Marxism-Leninism unlocked all the world's secrets, underrated the special skills which the intellectuals possessed. Not infrequently the intellectuals were assigned menial tasks, or not given any work at all. For their part, the intellectuals ridiculed the cadres, whom they considered ignorant, and often refused to participate in Party-led activities. The waste and inefficiency which characterized much of the 'socialist construction' under the First Five-Year Plan was convincing evidence that the cadres were making too many decisions of a technical nature. Eventually, the Western-oriented intellectuals inherited by the PRC could be replaced by technicians who might combine professional expertise with correct political views, but in the meantime fuller use would have to be made of the personnel available.

In January 1956 the Central Committee called a national meeting of CCP functionaries to consider the problem of how to reform and unite with the intellectuals. Addressing the meeting, Chou En-lai said that China was confronted with a scientific bottleneck due to the country's shortage of skilled people. He noted that there were nearly four million persons in the country classified as intellectuals. Most of them held government posts as doctors, teachers, and so on. Of the 100,000 'higher' intellectuals, whom he considered the key to the problem, he said that only about 45 per cent were 'progressive', while another 40 per cent had taken a fence-sitting position; only a few were really 'backward'. In what was to become a device to isolate the uncooperative elements, Chou proposed that more intellectuals be accepted as CCP members. Previously, applications for membership from intellectuals had seldom been approved, but during a one-year period from late 1956 to late 1957 the number of intellectuals in the Party jumped by 50 per cent. Chou also called upon Party cadres to improve their relations with non-Party intellectuals.

The attack on Stalin at the Twentieth Congress of the CPSU, which convened in Moscow in February 1957, directly influenced the unfolding of the Hundred Flowers campaign in China. The admission that Stalin had isolated himself from the people gave further impetus to the drive to rid the Party of the 'sectarian' attitudes which were stifling initiative among the intellectuals. The revelations of the CPSU Congress about the evils of Stalin's rule shattered the little world of Marxist-Leninist infallibility in which the CCP bureaucrats lived. Party members were human beings who could make mistakes. The CCP's official reaction to de-Stalinization was contained in an editorial entitled 'On the Historical Experience of the Dictatorship of the Proletariat', which appeared in the Peking *People's Daily* on 5 April 1956. Stalin had become 'conceited and impudent', it said, because he had lost touch with the masses; in Stalin's 'democratic centralism' there had been too much centralism and not enough democracy. To avoid similar mistakes, the editorial said, it was essential for the CCP to rely on the 'wisdom of the masses' lest it succumb to bureaucratization.

A month after the *People's Daily* editorial on de-Stalinization, Mao Tse-tung delivered a speech in which he called upon artists and writers to 'let a hundred flowers bloom' and upon scientists to 'let a hundred schools of thought contend'. Mao's speech was not published, but at the end of May the CCP's propaganda chief, Lu Ting-yi, made it clear that Mao wanted the intellectuals to voice their criticism of the regime. Blind obedience served no useful purpose. To encourage them to speak out, he observed that the only proper criterion for judging works of art was whether or not they served the working people as a whole. The intent of the Hundred Flowers campaign, as it came to be known, was to release the productive capacity of the intellectuals the better to serve China's socialist construction. In this respect the intellectuals as a class were lagging behind the other non-proletarian classes, whose 'socialist transformation' was, in the spring of 1956, nearing completion. Lu suggested that the cadres should help the intellectuals to raise their low Marxist-Leninist level, while the intellectuals should help the cadres to raise their low technical level. However, little blooming or contending occurred. At the Eighth Party Congress in September the leadership made it clear that it still was not satisfied. Not only were the intellectuals not speaking out, but the Party's 'style of work' was not improving. In particular, the 'doctrinaire' and 'sectarian' attitudes of the cadres threatened to separate the Party from the masses and to inhibit the intellectuals. The situation was made more urgent by the troubles in Poland and Hungary, and in November the Central Committee decided that a Party rectification campaign was essential. It was directed against 'the three evils' of bureaucracy, subjectivism, and sectarianism.

The official CCP reaction to the suppression of the Hungarian uprising by Soviet forces was expressed in 'More on the Historical Experience of the Dictatorship of the Proletariat', which appeared as an editorial in the Peking *People's Daily* on 29 December 1956. It carried forward some of the theses propounded in the editorial of 5 April and advanced a number of new propositions. The most important of these was the concept of contradictions within the ranks of the people in a socialist country. Because Stalin's rule had become doctrinaire, the CPSU had become cut off from the masses and Stalinism had been overthrown. Contradictions of a similar kind had developed in Hungary. Such contradictions could and must be overcome, but in doing so it is inadmissible, the editorial said, to attack the leadership of the Communist Party, the defender of the people against imperialism. That would be revisionism. The contradiction between the imperialist camp and the socialist camp is primary, or 'antagonistic' ('contradictions between the enemy and us'); contradictions among the people (between different groups) are secondary or 'non-antagonistic'. The editorial warned that the 'anti-doctrinaire tide' sweeping the socialist world must not be allowed to become revisionist.

Mao Tse-tung's speech, 'On the Correct Handling of Contradictions Among the People', delivered on 27 February 1957, was not published until June. In the interim, however, it was widely disseminated among responsible Party personnel to provide the guide lines for the campaign to rectify the Party's working style, which was formally proclaimed on 27 April. Only with the inauguration of the rectification campaign did the intellectuals finally speak out. For a year they had hesitated to respond to Lu Ting-yi's call to 'Let a hundred flowers bloom, let a hundred schools of thought contend'. Mao's 'Contradictions' speech had encouraged them, but by the time it was published, in June, the hundred flowers were being ploughed under. The 'blooming' and 'contending' was so virulently anti-Party that after only a few weeks it was cut short. It gave way to an 'anti-rightist' campaign which hit back at the Party's critics among the intellectuals. Apparently, the intellectuals had failed to heed Mao's advice that they distinguish between 'poisonous weeds' and 'fragrant flowers' (that is, between antagonistic and non-antagonistic contradictions).

In sum, the critics of the regime who ventured to express themselves in 1957 declared that the system itself was at fault and that under existing circumstances Party rectification was impossible. Since Liberation, the Party had become a fierce, inward-looking monster which thought only of its own preservation. The National People's Congress and the government administration constituted a façade behind which the Party actually wielded power. Only Party decisions were seriously implemented. Non-Party personnel were ignored: they had not been granted authority commensurate with the positions they held. Being all-powerful, the Party could ignore criticism and practice not only the 'three evils' which the rectification campaign was designed to eliminate (bureaucracy, subjectivism, sectarianism), but the traditional evils of Chinese bureaucracy as well. Of these, arrogance and nepotism were perhaps the most widespread: one critic called the rectification campaign 'a movement to alight from sedan chairs', while criticism of special privileges enjoyed by relatives of officials was common. It was charged that only optimistic reports were forwarded from lower to higher levels. There was no standard system of law enforcement. The various freedoms formally granted by the Constitution were frequently violated; local Party leaders readily turned themselves into potentates. The Party was less concerned with the fate of the country than with its own fate. It had become a new ruling class, representing a new tyranny. A second revolution was necessary. Toward the end of the Hundred Flowers episode the students, inflamed by the events in Hungary, became active. Student protest movements erupted in several cities and a number of officials were beaten. The students anticipated the cultural revolution of a decade later in calling for a second May Fourth. It is quite possible that Mao Tse-tung was personally responsible for launching the Hundred Flowers movement and that his opponents within the Central Committee were responsible for ending it.

The anti-rightist movement which began in the summer of 1957 was the antithesis of the rectification campaign which had given rise to it. It struck at conservative elements both inside and outside the Party, at the intellectuals who had been criticizing the Party and at their sympathizers among right-wing Party members. In many respects, it was a resumption of the 1955 campaign against 'counter-revolutionaries', the excesses of which had been widely denounced during the Hundred Flowers period. The distinction between 'counterrevolutionaries' and 'rightists' was extremely fuzzy. Moreover, sudden changes in the ideological climate could cause these categories to shift so as to embrace different ranges of opinion and activity. In Maoist phraseology, a 'non-antagonistic' contradiction could become an 'antagonistic' contradiction, so that what is legitimate today might be culpable tomorrow. In a speech of 26 June 1957, Chou En-lai said that right-wing elements were trying 'to drive our country from the path of socialism to the path of capitalism'. The Premier's address was made to the Fourth Session of the First National People's Congress and provided the keynote for the anti-rightist campaign. 'Confessions' of rightists were a prominent feature of this same NPC meeting.

The 'rightists' denounced in the summer of 1957 would have been considered radicals before 1949. Most of them, disgusted by the decadence of the Kuomintang, had become sympathetic toward the Communists, and a few of them had joined the Party after 1949. The core of the rightists was made up of members of the Democratic League, the party which had been proscribed by Chiang Kai-shek in 1947 after it attempted to take a middle position between the

Kuomintang and the Communists. Two leaders of the Democratic League, Chang Po-chün and Lo Lung-chi, became the principal scapegoats for the CCP, which had balked at being 'rectified'. Many of the 'rightists' associated with the 'Chang-Lo alliance' had been educated in Britain or the United States and were unable to accept unreservedly the new learning imported from the Soviet Union. For instance, Yale graduate Ma Yin-ch'u, now president of Peking University, clung to the 'reactionary' idea that excessive population growth could threaten China's economic development. In general, the 'rightists' were appalled by what they saw as the waste and inefficiency of 'socialist construction', the cruelty and arbitrariness of the state's persecution of 'counterrevolutionaries', and the ignorance and backwardness of the new class of Party bureaucrats. They felt that they had tried to cooperate with the revolution but had been rejected by it.

In the eyes of the Party, the anti-rightist campaign of 1957 was a socialist revolution on the political and ideological fronts comparable to the 1956 revolution on the economic front; it complemented and strengthened the victories in socialist transformation. The anti-rightist campaign was extended to factory and farm, and even to the military. The usual punishment meted out to rightists was reform through labour, as it is a firmly-held tenet of the CCP and Chairman Mao that participation in physical work is essential to ideological remoulding. Associated with the anti-rightist campaign was a socialist-education movement, aimed especially at the rural masses, which sought to strengthen belief in the superiority of socialism over capitalism. Capitalism was held to be still deeply entrenched in the countryside, where the middle peasants had staged a comeback at the expense of the cooperatives.

Writers in Communist China

When the People's Republic of China was established in 1949, all the major writers remained in China. These included such veteran leftists as Mao Tun, who now became Minister of Culture, and Kuo Mo-jo. Others who remained were merely 'progressive'—for instance, Pa Chin, whose novels of revolutionary youth were popular in the 1930s but were criticized by the Communists for their anarchist views. Lao She and other essentially non-political writers also chose to stay. Lao She had long criticized the old society, but his standpoint was humanitarian rather than political. He returned to China in

October 1949 from a protracted stay in the US. Armed with his life-long sympathy for the poor, he succeeded in writing works on the new regime—especially such plays as *Dragon Beard Ditch*—which are both ideologically 'correct' and popular as entertainment.

To be correct meant, and still means, to follow the principles laid down by Mao Tse-tung at Yenan in 1942. Literature must be written for the masses, from their standpoint, in language intelligible to them. At the First National Congress of Writers and Artists in July 1949 these ideas were reaffirmed. Chou Yang, a leading Communist liter-ary theorist for over two decades, praised various works written since 1942 which complied with Mao Tse-tung's criteria, including the opera *The White-Haired Girl* by Ho Ching-chih and Ting Yi; Chou Li-po's *Hurricane*; and Chao Shu-li's *Rhymes of Li Yu-tsai* and *Changes in Li Village*. In their use of simple form and language these works furthered Mao Tse-tung's aim of 'popularizing' literature, as did the use of 'national forms': folk-songs and simple verse inter-spersed in a novel, or traditional opera used as a vehicle for tales of class struggle. At the same time, there was a conscious debt to Soviet literature. Soviet literary theory was the source of the term 'social-ist realism', which Chou Yang laid down as the guiding principle for writers at the second writers' congress in 1953. Without differing from Mao Tse-tung's ideas, socialist realism strongly emphasizes the writer's duty to conform to the Party's current policies; to educate the people on these policies and their dependence on the Party; and to show the struggle of the heroic masses (led by the Party) against negative, backward elements as ever victorious. Chou Yang affirmed that *The White-Haired Girl* and the works of Chou Li-po and Chao Shu-li were works of socialist realism.

Organized into the All-China Federation of Literary and Art Workers, headed by Kuo Mo-Jo, and the Union of Chinese Writers, headed by Mao Tun, writers took part in the various Party campaigns in order to correct their views and learn from the masses. Lao She, for instance, wrote a play on the Five-Anti campaign and Pa Chin produced stories on the Korean War—both mentioned favourably by Chou Yang. Criticism and self-criticism were also employed to ex-pedite political remoulding.

There were, in addition, campaigns directed against specific literary targets. In the early years, Hu Shih's pragmatism, idealism, ideas on language reform and studies of classical Chinese literature were criticized. Hu Shih was not in China, but the campaign aimed to stamp out his influence: contributors to the volumes of criticism in-cluded many former students and colleagues. Hu Shih also came under attack in the *Dream of the Red Chamber* case. A critique of this eighteenth-century Chinese novel had been written by Yü P'ing-po in 1923 and re-issued in 1952. In 1954 Yü was attacked for not using Marxist criticism, which would begin with an historical-materialist analysis of the social context in which the *Dream of the Red Chamber* was written and then judge whether the novel was, for its time, a step forward in the revolutionary class struggle. Instead, Yü had em-ployed Hu Shih's 'incorrect' method, that of textual criticism. Yü also maintained that classical Chinese novels were written to enter-tain; but the Party insisted that the function of both the new and the old literature is (political) education and not entertainment.

Literary productivity in these early years was disappointing. Hu Feng attributed this to the subservience of literature to politics and to writers' participation in reform through labour. A Marxist of long standing, Hu accepted the Party's political leadership and aims, but he took issue with its control of literature. Ever since 1935 he had en-gaged in a running battle with the Communist literary authorities, notably Chou Yang. He believed that artistic truth is found in the writer's subjective response to objective reality; he could not accept the criteria of socialist realism. In July 1954, apparently believing he could change literary policy and so stimulate productivity, he aired his views in a memorandum to the CCP Central Committee. The Party had earlier hoped to reform him, but the campaign which fol-lowed was intended to eliminate his wrong ideas and his ambitions. Not only was his ideology rejected but he was accused of 'sectarian-ism'—that is, of wanting to gain literary leadership for his own fac-tion. Soon he was also accused of engaging in counterrevolutionary activities as an agent of the Kuomintang. He was expelled from the writers' associations in May 1955 and subsequently imprisoned.

This double accusation—of incorrect ideology and sectarianism—was repeated in many cases. For instance, Ting Ling, already criti-cized as petty-bourgeois in Yenan in 1942, came under attack in 1955 and in the anti-rightist campaign of 1957. Together with Ch'en Ch'i-hsia and others in the 'Ting-Ch'en clique', she was accused of harbouring such wrong tendencies as individualism and bourgeois humanism, and of defying Party control over literature. Her novel on land reform, *The Sun Shines over the Sangkan River*, had won a Stalin prize for literature in 1951 and was characterized as socialist realism by Chou Yang in 1952. Faults were now found in it, however, and a 1959 Communist literary history barely mentions it.

The official exuberance accompanying the introduction of communes and the Great Leap Forward in 1958 resulted in a new formula for literature: the combination of 'revolutionary realism and revolutionary romanticism'. Mao Tse-tung's poems—with their loving descriptions of the Chinese landscape as the setting for past and future victories of the revolution, and with their numerous allusions to Chinese myth, legend, and even classical literature—were declared excellent embodiments of this formula, which in turn served to justify their departure from socialist realism. Chinese mythological motifs were also widely used in the 'million poems movement' of 1957–59, the culmination of the movement for amateur literature begun by the Party in the 1930s. In this thoroughly Chinese 'Great Leap Forward in culture', 'the masses opened their lips', producing many millions of happy, optimistic, adulatory verses on Mao, the Party, and the new life—of the sort that professionals often found difficult to write. These were cultural symptoms of the Sino-Soviet split. With de-Stalinization, Soviet standards had been liberalized to such an extent that incorrect Chinese authors could find support for their ideas from correct Soviet authors. The anti-Soviet trend was later a factor in the downfall of Chou Yang, long the leading arbiter of China's literary doctrine, but also a great admirer of Soviet literature. In 1965, he was accused, among other things, of being 'a compradore, who could not open his mouth without citing foreigners'.

The nationalism and romanticism of this anti-Soviet period permitted the rehabilitation of much of the older literary heritage. Of the modern writers, only Lu Hsün has fully maintained his reputation. Despite his various battles with Communist literati during the decade preceding his death in 1936, he is revered both as a courageous revolutionary fighter and as a writer of socialist realism. On Taiwan, by contrast, Lu Hsün's works are banned, while other works of the Literary Revolution are either banned or out of print. Writers on Taiwan, with one or two exceptions, have produced nothing but shallow escapism. Without serious criticism there is a lack of literary standards, while the government, if it does not prescribe literary orthodoxy, does almost nothing to encourage writers.

CHAPTER SEVEN

Veering away from Moscow

The Great Leap Forward

Despite its vigorous appearance, the Chinese economy was in serious trouble at the end of the First Five-Year Plan. There were signs that, as the momentum generated by the Plan spent itself, the country would come to rest in a state of low-level equilibrium. Application of the Soviet model to China had indeed led to striking advances in industry, and particularly heavy industry, but this achievement had failed to stimulate rapid growth in the countryside. The rural economy was still characterized by handicrafts and traditional agricultural techniques. Agriculture was virtually stagnant, and the state was dependent upon agriculture both for capital accumulation and for industrial raw materials. Despite the fact that investment in the rural sector had risen from a projected level of 7·6 per cent of total investment under the First Five-Year Plan to an actual level of 10 per cent, the increase in agricultural output had been disappointingly small. Moreover, the peasants were consuming much of what increase had been achieved: they were eating the surplus intended for capital investment. The level of grain deliveries to the state, in taxes and in sales at fixed prices, had remained virtually stationary during the period of the First Five-Year Plan. The low priority accorded light industry under the Plan had led to an insufficiency of consumer goods, causing the peasants to withhold grain which might otherwise have been marketed. There were instances, too, of whole cooperatives retaining excessive quantities of grain by reporting a lower level of production than had actually been achieved. Meanwhile, urban population was increasing much faster than rural population: between 1952 and 1957 the urban increase was 30 per cent as compared with 9 per cent for rural population. More farm produce had to be transferred from country to town if urban standards of living were to be maintained. The question of how to bring about a substantial increase in agricultural production so as to increase deliveries to the state was the main preoccupation of China's leaders in the second half of 1957.

A retreat to free-market conditions was not the answer. The socialist education movement which swept China's rural areas during the summer of 1957 reached its climax in September with the discontinuation of limited free markets. This concession to capitalism, introduced a year earlier, permitted the farmer to sell his surplus product on the open market, but it encouraged him to concentrate his energies on the small private plots, with perhaps a few pigs and fruit trees, which he had been permitted to retain after cooperativization. There was no doubt that the private plots and limited free markets had contributed to the relative improvement of agriculture in 1957 as compared with 1956 and, in particular, to the recovery of pig production: in 1956 China's hog population stood at 84 million, compared with 90 million in 1952, but in 1957 it rose to 125 million. Pigs are important not only for food, pork being the most commonly consumed meat in China, but also for fertilizer, since pig manure is a prime source of crop nutrients for Chinese agriculture. The trouble with the private plots was that they encouraged the very capitalist tendencies and rich-peasant mentality which the CCP was determined to extirpate from the countryside. Private plots were banned in 1958 as the Great Leap Forward got under way. Even if the private plots and the limited free markets had remained, they could scarcely have solved China's agricultural dilemma, for they accounted for only a tiny fraction of the produce grown and marketed. The problem was to increase per-*mou* (1 *mou* = approximately one-sixth of an acre) yields in the cooperatives. This was the main burden of the Twelve-Year Plan for agriculture of January 1956 and of many subsequent reports. In his September 1957 'Report on the Rectification Campaign', Politburo-member Teng Hsiao-p'ing said bluntly that only when the per-*mou* yield in the cooperatives surpassed that realized by the rich peasants would the superiority of the socialist road over the capitalist road be clearly established, the implication being that this was not yet the case.

Teng's 'Report' was delivered to the third plenum of the Eighth Central Committee, which met from 20 September to 9 October

1957. By the time the plenum was adjourned, the radical views of the Central Committee's chairman, Mao Tse-tung, had won the day. The 'conservative' line embodied in the Second Five-Year Plan, which called for a continuation of Soviet-style planning, was rejected. Mao believed that social mobilization could be a substitute for material incentives in achieving higher output, and that investments of labour could be a substitute for investments of capital. Mao clearly shared the view expressed earlier by the Minister of Agriculture, Liao Lu-yen, that the fact that five-sixths of China's 600,000,000 people were peasants was a 'special feature' of China's industrialization. By emphasizing labour rather than capital, the heavy investments—as for the expansion of chemical-fertilizer output—which a more conventional approach would entail, could be avoided. Moreover, labour-intensive projects, notably in irrigation works, could yield immediate results. It was hoped that agricultural output could be expanded without slowing the pace of industrialization: this came to be called 'walking on two legs'. The triumph of Mao's views may have been aided by the launching of the Sputnik artificial satellite by the Soviet Union on 4 October, five days before the conclusion of the Central Committee plenum. When the commune movement, closely associated with the Great Leap Forward, began in 1958, the first people's commune to be formed was called the 'Sputnik commune'.

The Great Leap Forward was accompanied by a vast movement of administrative decentralization in which authority was transferred from the central people's government to the provinces, and from the government ministries to the provincial CCP committees. As early as the 1956 Eighth Party Congress it had been recognized that Soviet planning methods were too highly centralized for Chinese conditions, and that more local initiative should be permitted. During the Great Leap Forward 'the simultaneous development of central and regional industry' was another aspect of the policy of 'walking on two legs'. The decentralization decisions taken at the third plenum greatly enhanced the planning authority of the provinces, where the government was overshadowed by the Party. In accordance with their increased planning role, the provinces were allowed to retain a larger share of tax receipts. Decentralization was accompanied by an anti-rightist purge, which struck the provincial CCP committees in December 1957. Only the largest enterprises remained under the authority of the central government; virtually all of China's light industry was entrusted to the provinces, which even gained a measure of control over railroads. The share of industry under central authority fell from 46 per cent in 1957 to 27 per cent in 1958; correspondingly, the share under local authority rose from 54 to 73 per cent. The idea behind this downward transfer of authority was that, since 80 per cent of the raw materials for light industry came from the agricultural sector, agriculture and light industry could best be developed together in the provinces, while heavy industry—still the backbone of the economy—remained under central authority. It was hoped that by giving fuller play to local initiative the country's light industry, the link between town and country, would expand rapidly. Associated with this aspect of localism, the Great Leap Forward included a strong do-it-yourself element. Perhaps greater enthusiasm at the local level would help to compensate for the drying up of Soviet credits. No new credits were announced on the occasion of Chairman Mao's second visit to the Soviet Union, in the autumn of 1957, when he attended the fortieth anniversary celebrations of the October Revolution. Moreover, the earlier credits were now falling due: beginning in 1957 the PRC would, for the first time, be obliged to generate an overall export surplus.

The celebrations in Moscow were marked by expressions of confidence in the capacity of the socialist system to win a race of 'peaceful competition' with the West. The Russians made known their determination to overtake the United States, while the Chinese declared that in 15 years their economy would surpass Britain's. Soviet space accomplishments and a concurrent recession in the US filled the Chinese with confidence. They joined the Russians in castigating the Yugoslav revisionists for compromising with imperialism. Thus, it appeared that the Chinese could count on a favourable international situation in which to carry out their Great Leap Forward, and that, by generating a powerful revolutionary upsurge at home, they could succeed in bringing within reach their dearest external goal, the liberation of Taiwan.

The Great Leap Forward was several months old by the time it was first formulated in a systematic way. It was endorsed by the National People's Congress in February 1958. Further elaboration was provided by Liu Shao-ch'i's work report of 5 May 1958, delivered to the Second Session of the Eighth National Congress of the CCP. Postulated in ideological terms, the Great Leap coincided with a phase of the Chinese revolution called the 'construction of socialism', the successor to the 'transition to socialism' which had been basically completed by the end of 1956. The rectification campaign and the anti-rightist struggle of 1957 had prepared the way for the new revolutionary period. Liu noted that the objective of the Party's 'general line for socialist construction' was 'to build our country, in the shortest possible time, into a great socialist country with a modern industry, modern agriculture, and modern science and culture'. Liu expressed the Maoist concept of psychological mobilization of the people, which, it was hoped, would provide a substitute for material incentives:

> The broad masses of the working people have realized more fully that individual and immediate interests depend on and are bound up with collective and long-term interests and that the happiness of the individual lies in the realization of the lofty socialist ideals of all the people. That is why they have displayed in their work an heroic communist spirit of self-sacrifice. Their slogan is: 'Hard work for a few years, happiness for a thousand.' This mighty torrent of communist ideas has swept away many stumbling blocks—individualism, departmentalism, localism, and nationalism. In city and countryside, people vie with each other in joining in all kinds of voluntary labour. . . .

The Great Leap Forward had already achieved notable results by the time Liu spoke. He said that between October 1957 and April 1958 the irrigated area had been increased more than during the preceding eight years. To accomplish this work, tens of millions of peasants had been mobilized; they were reinforced by millions of city folk sent down to the villages in the *hsia-fang* ('back to the farm') movement. The total value of industrial output during the first four months of 1958 was reportedly 26 per cent higher than during the corresponding period of 1957. The decentralized planning introduced at the beginning of the Great Leap Forward came more and more to resemble anarchy as Party cadres everywhere sought to maximize output regardless of demand and cost. Production targets were constantly revised upward, as is indicated in the following example for steel, which was considered the prime indicator of success.

1958 target for steel output (millions of tons)				*Second Five-Year Plan ('62)*
In Feb.	*In March*	*In May*	*In Aug.*	*Target*
6·2	7	8–8·5	10·7	10·5–12

During 1958 steel was emphasized more than any other item. Under the slogan 'all people to iron and steel', small-scale, 'backyard' furnaces were set up all over the country. An enormous expansion of output resulted but the statistics for 1958 and 1959 were so inflated—as the Party itself later admitted—that comparisons are difficult to make. It does appear, however, that total investment and total industrial output expanded as much in the two years 1958–59 as in the preceding five. The enthusiasm said to have been generated by the Party's 'general line for socialist construction' was not the only reason for such dramatic growth. The 1958 agricultural crop was the largest ever harvested in China and, while the new irrigation works no doubt contributed to this success, the unusually favourable weather conditions which prevailed over most of the country during the year were even more important. Another important factor was the completion in 1958 of an unusually large number of the major Soviet-aided industrial plants begun during the First Five-Year Plan. By 1960 the modern industrial sector probably accounted for nearly 90 per cent of the value of China's total industrial output. As before, the industrial advance was led by heavy industry, while much of the increased output of light industry had to be exported to pay for the higher volume of machinery and industrial raw materials required by the Great Leap Forward.

Under the slogan 'let politics take command' CCP cadres took direct control of the Chinese economy during the Great Leap Forward. Managers and technicians were pushed aside; they were often made to engage in manual labour in farm or factory. Manual labour on the part of white-collar workers was one of the great fads of the Great Leap period. Mao thereby hoped to eliminate the 'contradiction' between mental and physical labour. Mao himself participated in the construction of a reservoir near Peking during the winter of 1958–59. This attempt to eliminate the dichotomy between mental and physical labour, together with the decentralization of decision-making, soon led to serious dislocations in the economy. Local shortages and surpluses of food, manufactured goods, and industrial raw materials occurred as the transport system fell farther and farther behind the demands put on it by the Great Leap Forward. The poor quality of industrial output became even more of a problem than it had been during the First Five-Year Plan. In 1960 the several thousand Russian technicians who had been engaged in the construction of industrial plants in China returned home, taking with them the blueprints for the new enterprises. Their departure, occasioned by ideological feuding between Moscow and Peking, was a serious blow to China's programme of industrialization and scientific research. The situation on the agricultural front was also bad. The 1959 crop was poor and the 1960 crop worse still. The per capita output of food crops, taking 1957 as 100, fell from the 112 attained in 1958 to 88 in 1959 and to 81 in 1960, China's most critical year since Liberation. Maternity wards, even in Peking, were not adequately provisioned, and military rations had to be cut. In December 1960 the PRC began buying wheat on the world market. The poor harvests, resulting from disasters of nature and of administration, contributed to the industrial slow-down. Industrial output tumbled by approximately 75 per cent in 1961 as compared with the peak output attained by the Great Leap Forward in 1959–60. The Great Leap Forward was terminated in January 1961 by a plenary session of the CCP Central Committee.

Communes

People's communes were the organizational complement of the Great Leap Forward. At the same time, they filled other organizational requirements independent of the needs of the Great Leap Forward and so remained after the Leap itself had been abandoned. People's communes—in fact if not in name—were organized during the winter of 1957–58 as a scheme for mobilizing labour on a sufficiently large scale for carrying out water conservancy and irrigation projects. Between the autumn harvest of 1957 and the spring ploughing of 1958 an estimated 100 million peasants were mobilized throughout the country to construct water-works needed for the expansion of agriculture. Responsibility for these projects was generally left to the agricultural producers' cooperatives. Usually, a number of APCs shared a common drainage system and therefore had common tasks with respect to irrigation. By joining forces they could also make more rational use of their man-power. Suggestions to this effect were probably filtering down through Party channels following a secret Politburo meeting in December 1957 which is believed to have decided upon the Great Leap Forward and the amalgamation of cooperatives into larger units.

The first commune to be accorded formal recognition as such was the 'Sputnik commune' in Honan province, institutionalized in April 1958. By the end of August virtually all the peasant households in the province had been communized, with 38,470 APCs being merged to form 1,378 communes. A Politburo meeting of August 1958 called for the adoption of the commune system throughout the country. In the main, this was accomplished by the end of the year. In 1959 there were approximately 24,000 communes with an average of 5,000 households per commune, accounting altogether for 99 per cent of China's peasant population. During 1960 and 1961 the number of communes was increased to over 70,000 as their average size dropped below 2,000 households: this brought them into rough correspondence with the rural township, or *hsiang*. Further adjustments were made so as to make this correspondence precise.

The highest producing unit, the commune, was thus merged with the lowest unit of administration, the *hsiang*. This fusion of government and society was hailed as the beginning of communism. The *hsiang* people's congress and *hsiang* people's council now became organs of the commune, but this transition actually placed all power in the hands of the Party. The CCP had been patiently developing its strength in the *hsiang* ever since the land-reform campaign a decade earlier. With the APCs, introduced in 1955, it had attempted to extend its authority down to the level of the natural village, or *ts'un*. This effort had been largely balked, partly by the strong ties, mainly of kinship, which bound together members of the *ts'un*, and partly by the strong influence still exerted by the wealthier peasants, who generally opposed the collectives. The extreme localism at the *ts'un* level, which no previous government in China had even attempted to challenge, was the reason for the failure of collectivization to make appreciably larger quantities of agricultural produce available to the state. It was hoped that in the commune movement *ts'un* barriers would be broken down and the authority of the Party extended into the natural village. Party branches at the *hsiang* level were directly dependent upon the Party committee at the *hsien*, or county, level; these *hsien* committees were, in turn, subordinate to the provincial Party committees, which had been made all-powerful by the administrative decentralization of 1957. Consequently, the creation of communes gave the Party an unprecedented degree of authority over rural life in China.

Just as the cooperative movement had been carried out within the framework of the *hsiang*, communization took place within the framework of the *hsien*. It was expected that, within each *hsien*, the communes would form federations which would gradually merge with the *hsien* administration. This did not occur. Instead, centralization remained concentrated at the commune level; indeed, by the end of 1958 there was some devolution of authority back to the brigade level. Within the commune there were three levels of ownership and responsibility: commune, brigade, and team. The agricultural producers' cooperatives (APCs) became the production brigades of the communes. At first, when the commune comprised an average of 30 production brigades, the Party attempted to mobilize labour on a commune-wide basis and to make the commune the unit of accounting, both for production and wages. But, unlike the APC, or production brigade, the commune was so large that it was difficult for the peasant to identify with it. He was turned into a proletarian, simply receiving a wage for the performance of whatever work was assigned to him. Separated from the familiar surroundings of his village, he found his work more and more tedious. Something like military discipline was introduced into the commune, and the Party tried to make the peasant identify with an impersonal producing unit rather than with a familiar group. Under the slogan 'everyone a soldier', the people's militia, which had been inactive since the early years of the regime, was reintroduced in September 1958 to meet a serious situation in the Taiwan straits and a possible Nationalist invasion. Once the crisis had passed, the militia units became shock troops on the production front.

During the summer of 1958 a labour shortage developed in the Chinese countryside. In addition to the demands of water conservancy works, the Central Committee had called for the development of small-scale industries at the local level. This would make it possible for the communes to take fuller advantage of locally available labour and raw materials. The *hsien* were given primary responsibility for the development of such small-scale industries. Coal, iron, and steel production were given first priority. Above the *hsien*, at the provincial level, were the larger enterprises, usually producing consumer goods, which had been transferred from central to provincial control in late 1957. Below the *hsien*, at the commune level, an enormous spurt of handicraft and workshop production took place during the years of the Great Leap Forward. Urged by the Party to exert themselves to the utmost, producing units at all three levels sought to expand production as rapidly as possible. So many peasants were drawn into factories and workshops that the agricultural labour force was seriously weakened. In 1960 a mass campaign—'everyone to grain and cotton'—had to be launched in order to bring back sufficient labour to the agricultural front. Meanwhile, the Party sought to mobilize women for productive work. It was the effort to 'liberate' women from 'the fetters of household chores' which set in motion the attempt to centre life within the commune around the individual rather than the family. Commune kitchens, mess halls, nurseries, and kindergartens were all designed to enable women to join the men on the production front. There is reason to believe that this movement was more unpopular with the men than with the women.

The ideal of the commune was to unite working and living by making the communes self-sufficient in their basic daily requirements. What they were unable to produce in the way of manufactured goods was to be supplied as much as possible by the *hsien* and province rather than by the large-scale enterprises which remained under central control. In this way, economic development became the concern of the locality as much as of the nation. Such decentralization was more in keeping with China's traditionally compartmentalized life than with Soviet planning techniques. But, for the communes to succeed, rural life had to be modernized. Electrification is one measure of communal modernization, and modernization is impossible without irrigation, mechanization, chemical fertilizers. The rationalization of the rural economy, expressed in these terms, continued long after the communal mess halls and other extreme features of the Great Leap Forward had been abandoned.

An attempt to extend the commune system to urban areas began in the autumn of 1958; it was suspended in December and then briefly resumed during the winter of 1959–60. Like the rural communes, the urban communes were designed to bring working and living into a more harmonious relationship. A characteristic feature of the urban communes were the 'street industries', run for the most part by women 'liberated' from household chores. The chaos resulting from the policy of 'let politics take command' spread from the countryside to the cities as Party cadres assumed management functions in industry. Private enjoyment receded from daily life as mass movements monopolized leisure time. In June 1960 it was claimed that about 80 per cent of the urban population had been communized, but when the Great Leap Forward subsided in the following year the life of the urban people's communes was extinguished, leaving scarcely any trace. Unlike the rural communes—which, for instance, proved their worth in fighting the floods and droughts of 1959 and 1960—the urban communes served no real social or economic purpose.

On 10 December 1958, the Central Committee endorsed a resolution which served to check the excessive enthusiasm displayed by many cadres in the early stages of rural communization. The cadres were told that the attempt to collectivize homes, chickens, small tools, and other personal belongings was wrong; they were reminded that China was still in the stage of socialism and that Communism could not be introduced prematurely. The scope of the communes was further restricted by the decisions of the eighth plenum of the Central Committee which met in August 1959. An order issued by the plenum altered the relationship among commune, brigade, and team in favour of the last two. In effect, a process of decentralization took place within the commune, which had been proven so unwieldy and impersonal as to hurt overall efficiency and individual initiative. In the same month Premier Chou En-lai introduced the slogan 'the whole country is a single chessboard', to dramatize the fact that administrative decentralization had gone too far. At its ninth plenum in January 1961, the Central Committee delivered the *coup de grâce* to the Great Leap Forward, but the rural communes survived. Their continued vitality reflects the regime's refusal to allow urbanization to run its course in China as it has in other countries in the process of rapid economic development. People must stay in the countryside and become more productive there, instead of migrating to the cities. Stringent regulations were introduced in 1957 to check the flow of population from rural to urban areas, a flow which had been largely responsible for the rise in China's urban population from 58 million in 1949 to 89 million in 1956. In 1958–59 a process of forced de-urbanization set in as millions of city dwellers were sent back to the countryside, where they could be more economically fed, clothed, and housed.

The Sino-Soviet split

Differences between Moscow and Peking, openly aired by 1960, created a deep schism in the international Communist movement. But the pre-existing relations between the two largest Communist states had not been perfectly harmonious, nor were their subsequent relations completely discordant. Two decades of Sino-Soviet friction, caused by the fact that Stalin's presuppositions about China were frequently proved wrong, preceded the CCP's victory in 1949. The Sino-Soviet alliance of February 1950 was based on cold calculation on both sides; it was not characterized by really warm feelings between the Russian and Chinese peoples. The death of Stalin in March 1953 did not immediately affect the alliance, except to heighten, for a time, Mao Tse-tung's personal prestige within the Communist bloc. Friendship with the Soviet Union was written into the PRC Constitution, adopted in September 1954. Moscow, especially after the ascendancy of Khrushchev in February 1955, came to acknowledge China's co-leadership status within the bloc. From the Twentieth Soviet Party Congress onward, however, the issues on which agreement could not be reached began to loom larger than those on which agreement was possible.

The harmony that had existed in 1954–55 between Peking and Moscow, with regard to both East-West and intra-bloc relations, gave way to discord in 1956–57. The Soviet Union's development of thermonuclear weapons in 1953 had led to the espousal of peaceful coexistence by Premier Malenkov, who declared in March 1954 that war would mean the end of civilization. The Chinese agreed with the Russians that the optimum policy in a situation of strategic balance would be one of peaceful competition, especially in the countries which lay on the periphery of the Soviet bloc. It was at this time that Peking enunciated its 'Five Principles of Peaceful Coexistence' and put them to good use at the 1955 Afro-Asian conference. The strong backing which Peking enjoyed in the form of the Soviet Union's hydrogen-bomb capability—dramatized by a series of very large H-bomb tests in the autumn of 1955—was matched by a greater degree of independence within the bloc than China had previously enjoyed. In short, Peking was in an optimum situation. Polycentrism within a Soviet bloc strongly united against the West enhanced the PRC's strength without hindering her freedom of action. Thus, Peking did not demur when Khrushchev dismissed V. M. Molotov, Stalin's tough-minded foreign minister, and brought about a reconciliation with Tito in May 1955.

The loosening of bloc ties which followed Khrushchev's denunciation of Stalin at the Twentieth CPSU Congress in January 1956 became a problem for Peking only when it threatened bloc unity, as it did in Budapest in November. For his own reasons, Khrushchev could not tolerate the independent line to which Tito soon reverted, and at the November 1957 meeting of Communist parties, which convened in Moscow on the occasion of the fortieth anniversary of the October Revolution, Mao joined Khrushchev in denouncing revisionism. His theory of antagonistic and non-antagonistic contradictions provided the only theoretical analysis of intra-bloc relations available at the time, since Khrushchev did not advance one of his own. According to Mao's thesis, contradictions within the bloc are non-antagonistic, while contradictions between bloc states and imperialist states are antagonistic. Mao's position as a Marxist-Leninist thinker was acknowledged at the November meeting. Mao took advantage of his platform in Moscow not only to appeal for bloc unity but also to advocate a shift in bloc policy toward the West.

The successful test-firing of an intercontinental ballistic missile (ICBM) by the Russians in August 1957, followed by the Sputnik earth satellite in the autumn, indicated to the Chinese that the world balance of forces had shifted in favour of the Soviet bloc. Mao declared in November that the international situation had reached 'a new turning point' marked by the fact that 'the East wind prevails over the West wind'. The Chinese thought that the Soviet bloc had achieved a strategic advantage—very likely a temporary one—which ought to be vigorously exploited. The Russians were much more cautious. While admitting that their achievements in rocketry had enhanced their position vis-à-vis the West, they did not believe that the Soviet bloc could enjoy an absolute superiority over the West until the Soviet economy had outstripped that of the United States. The Russians seemed to be as terrified by their new ICBM as they had been four years earlier by their first hydrogen bombs. Instead of developing a more militant policy, as Peking urged, the Russians looked for negotiations with the West on outstanding issues, in the hope that their new power would improve their bargaining position. Moscow's call for a summit meeting put the Soviet Union on the negotiating trail which led to the Eisenhower–Khrushchev meeting in 1959 and to the Sino-Soviet split. By the time of the November 1960 Moscow conference of 81 Communist parties, Peking had pinned the 'revisionist' label on Khrushchev himself and was actively campaigning to form an anti-Soviet bloc of Communist parties.

The main reason for Peking's inability to follow Moscow's lead in seeking an accommodation with the West was United States intervention in the Chinese civil war, in the form of its alliance with Taiwan. The *status quo* was not acceptable to Peking, as it apparently was to Moscow. In the Taiwan straits crisis of 1958 the Russians were to demonstrate that they would not risk a conflict with the United States on behalf of Chinese irredentism.

Not only would the Russians not risk war over Taiwan, they would not risk war at all. General war, which would mean the 'end of civiliz-ation', was not acceptable, and any local war, by a process of escala-tion, could lead to general war. As early as the Twentieth Party Con-gress the Russians had intimated that they would not support wars of national liberation. This approach, with its corollary, that Communist parties should attain power by parliamentary means, was denounced by Peking with increasing vehemence. In the Chinese view, refusal to risk war was tantamount to capitulation. They said that local wars were inevitable and that the risk of general war had to be taken. Wars of national liberation, according to Peking, were 'just' wars and had to be supported, while 'unjust' wars launched by the imperialists were to be opposed. 'We oppose war but we do not fear it', was a slogan which appeared in Chinese journals during the debate over strategy. The Russians countered with the idea that war had been outmoded by technology, bolstering their case with obscure quota-tions from Lenin.

After 1956 the Russians did not expect, and probably did not desire, the seizure of power by Communist parties by means of armed revolution. Not only were the risks of war considered too great, but Moscow valued its relations with most of the governments—such as Nasser's in Egypt—against which 'wars of national liberation' might be directed. It proposed, instead, that the Soviet bloc should assist bourgeois democratic states in evolving peacefully into socialist states. In a declaration issued by the Conference of 81 Communist parties which met in Moscow at the end of 1960, the states considered most ready and likely to make the transition from bourgeois to socialist states were referred to as 'national democracies'. A 'national demo-cracy' was described as a state which eschewed military alliances with the West and allowed democratic political activity at home. The very example of the successes achieved by the Soviet bloc was sup-posed to propel such states in the direction of socialism, with the Communists finally coming to power by parliamentary means. The Chinese were quick to point out that this policy was reminiscent of the disastrous policy pursued by the Comintern in China during the 1920's; 'national democratic' states were more likely to persecute their Communist parties than to allow them to take over the reins of government.

According to Peking, the policy needed in the zone of uncommitted states between the Eastern and Western camps was one of 'protracted conflict'. 'Protracted conflict' was a corollary of the 'permanent revolution' which provided the ideological backdrop for the Great Leap Forward. The concept of 'permanent revolution' had already proved an embarrassment to the Russians, who had every appearance of having given up revolution altogether. 'Protracted conflict' was equally embarrassing, for it laid bare the extent of Moscow's fear of war and its corresponding reluctance to support revolutions in the underdeveloped countries of Asia, Africa, and Latin America. Khrushchev declared placidly at the Twenty-first Soviet Party Congress in 1959 that, since the socialist bloc was becoming stronger and stronger, the ultimate victory of socialism throughout the world was assured. Thus, he felt no compunction about seeking a détente with the West. The PRC became increasingly concerned about the possibility of an arms control agreement between Moscow and Washington, and in the spring of 1960 castigated Khrushchev for 'revising, emasculating, and betraying' Leninism. The only option remaining for China was to attempt to substitute its own leadership for that of the Soviet Union over the world revolutionary movement. In order to support this movement, as well as to ensure the attainment of her own goals, China needed a nuclear capability of her own.

Taiwan and the PLA

Excluding purely domestic concerns, Taiwan has continued to be the most serious political problem facing the People's Republic of China. It symbolizes the continuation of the Chinese civil war, while United States involvement in that struggle has provided a guarantee of continuing hostility between Washington and Peking. The interjection of US naval forces between Taiwan and the mainland in 1950 prevented a planned attack on the island by the People's Liberation Army; these forces remained on duty in the Taiwan straits during and after the Korean War. The refusal of the United Nations to seat a Communist Chinese delegation helped to perpetuate the myth that the refugee Nationalist government on Taiwan was the government of all China. There is agreement between Peking and Taipei on one issue: that the Nationalist government cannot claim to be the government of Taiwan alone, for the status of the island as a province of China has never been questioned by either side. Thus, both sides have furiously rejected a so-called 'two-Chinas' solution which would provide for a state of Taiwan independent of Peking. Neither the Soviet Union nor the United States has wished to become involved in a shooting war to uphold the claims of its protégé. Washington has made it clear to Chiang Kai-shek that, as a condition attached to US military aid to Taiwan, the US government must be consulted prior to any military move against the mainland, while the Russians have refused to give Peking the all-out nuclear backing which the Chinese consider essential for the liberation of Taiwan by the PLA. There has been resentment on both sides against the restraining hand of the respective benefactors, but this has not been sufficient to drive Taipei and Peking together.

In addition to Taiwan, the Nationalists continue to hold a number of off-shore islands situated so close to the mainland as to raise serious doubts on both sides as to whether they can be considered in the same way as Taiwan, 100 miles from the Chinese coast. Chinese Communist attacks on these islands caused tense situations in 1954–55 and in 1958. A sea and air attack on one of the island groups, the Tachens, had succeeded by January 1955 in forcing the Nationalist garrison to withdraw. The withdrawal was assisted by US forces. The US–Taiwan Mutual Defense Treaty, signed in December 1954, was ratified in March 1955. The Soviet Union showed much less determination. On a visit to Peking in September 1954, when the offensive against the Tachens was beginning, Khrushchev made clear Moscow's reluctance to be drawn into any fracas over Taiwan. In February 1955, N. A. Bulganin, with whom Khrushchev shared power, reaffirmed Moscow's support for Peking's legal position with respect to Taiwan, but there was no new Soviet commitment to match the US–Taiwan treaty. The Russians tacitly accepted the *status quo* in the Taiwan straits, much to the chagrin of Peking. The pattern of events in 1958 virtually duplicated that of 1954–55, the PLA initiative being accompanied by cautious Soviet statements; once the danger of conflict had passed, the Soviet tone became more threatening.

Speaking to the National People's Congress in February 1958, Chou En-lai omitted the usual qualifier 'peacefully' in referring to China's determination to liberate Taiwan. The Taiwan situation was probably taken up by the Military Committee of the CCP Central Committee when it met three months later to review China's overall military posture. This unusual meeting, which began late in May and lasted into July 1958, was followed, at the end of July, by a three-day visit to Peking by Khrushchev. The purpose of Khrushchev's visit was undoubtedly to warn China against rash action in the Taiwan straits. As if to underscore the absence of any Soviet commitment, the communiqué of 3 August issued on Khrushchev's departure did not even refer to Taiwan. During the next two to three weeks, statements from Moscow were pacific in tone; those from Peking, bellicose. On 23 August the Chinese Communists began a heavy bombardment of Quemoy, at the mouth of Amoy harbour. The intent of the PLA was to blockade the island by means of artillery fire, thereby forcing its surrender. A rapid build-up of US forces in the area indicated, however, that this would not be acceptable in Taipei or Washington. On 4 September, Secretary of State Dulles declared that the United States would help defend Quemoy if the Nationalist garrison became hard pressed. The PRC backed down two days later when Chou En-lai indicated Peking's willingness to resume the ambassadorial talks in Warsaw which had earlier been held with the US. On 7 September, the day after this retreat, Khrushchev stated in a letter to Eisenhower that an attack on the PRC would be an attack on the Soviet Union. The blockade of Quemoy was soon broken, thanks in part to the use of US warships to escort supply vessels en route from Taiwan, and in late September the PLA suffered a further reverse when its Soviet-designed MIG jets were outgunned by American F-86 jets flown by Chinese Nationalists. In one day, 24 September, ten MIGs were shot down over the Taiwan straits. On 6 October the PRC Minister of Defence, P'eng Teh-huai, ordered a suspension of the bombardment of Quemoy and offered to negotiate with Taiwan. The heavy concentration of US forces, equipped with nuclear weapons, in the Taiwan straits made the Russians fearful that a war might begin accidentally. Moscow remained extremely cautious. Peking, by contrast, was moved to publish, under the title 'Imperialists and All Reactionaries Are Paper Tigers', a special collection of bellicose statements from the writings of Mao Tse-tung.

The 1958 PLA initiative in the Taiwan straits was probably designed, with Soviet concurrence, as a probing action to test US responses. Had the global balance of power shifted now that the Soviet Union had ICBMs? The firm American reaction to the shelling of Quemoy seemed to confirm the Soviet hypothesis that Moscow's enhanced rocket capability had had but a marginal effect on the balance of power—no radical shift had occurred. In particular, the Soviet ICBM, capable of striking directly at US targets, did not appear to have affected US readiness to threaten the use of tactical nuclear weapons.

Undoubtedly, the Chinese also looked upon the action in the Taiwan straits as a way of probing Soviet intentions. By 1954, the PRC's military leaders had become aware of the important role which nuclear weapons might play in future wars and of China's corresponding military dependence on the Soviet Union. The 1958 Taiwan straits episode demonstrated Moscow's reluctance to provide military backing for purely Chinese ventures. Because China did not herself possess nuclear weapons, therefore, Moscow exerted an inordinate degree of influence over Chinese military planning. Peking had already decided to construct her own nuclear weapons and to commit to this enterprise the enormous resources required. The failure to take Quemoy may have served to silence any opposition within the PLA to the decision to develop a Chinese nuclear capability as well as any disagreements over means to this end.

In September 1959, just a year after the Taiwan straits crisis, a thoroughgoing shakeup occurred in China's military command structure. Defence Minister P'eng Teh-huai was replaced by Lin Piao and changes were made in other key posts as well. A dispute probably arose over the defence policy to be adopted during the period, of approximately ten years, between the decision to construct nuclear weapons and the attainment of a nuclear capability. The shakeup in the military high command suggests that it had been decided not to divert resources from priority economic requirements for extensive re-equipping of the PLA during this transition period, in the course of which the military would have to rely more on ideology than on weapons: 'Let politics take command!' applied as much to the military as to the economy during the Great Leap Forward. China's military vulnerability during this transition period may have been one reason for the commune movement, with its characteristic process of de-urbanization, while the Great Leap itself may have been called into being in part to insure the mobilization of the resources required for the nuclear programme. The 1959 personnel changes reflect the desire of the Party to ensure that, during this critical period, political factors take priority over purely professional considerations in the nation's defence structure.

One rationalization offered for the 1958 Taiwan straits fiasco was that the capture of Quemoy without the liberation of Taiwan itself, presently beyond the grasp of the PLA, would have facilitated the emergence of 'two Chinas'. Nationalist control of the off-shore islands, situated well within China's territorial waters, provided some insurance that Taiwan would not be set up as an independent political entity. If anything, the Nationalists were even more opposed to a 'two-Chinas' policy than were the Communists, for they would have no political legitimacy in an independent Taiwan. Discussion in the UN and elsewhere of a possible 'two-Chinas' solution had coincided with a recrudescence of the Taiwanese nationalist movement which demanded self-determination. Such freedom of the press as existed on Taiwan was suppressed by a new law introduced in June 1958. In 1960, in the notorious Lei Chen case, a publisher was jailed on charges of treason after he had questioned the feasibility of invading the mainland.

Indonesia and Japan

Indonesia and Japan comprise island groups even more distant from the Chinese mainland than Taiwan. Their insular position has largely shaped their relations with the PRC. Unlike those states which have common frontiers with China, Indonesia and Japan have not been forced to declare themselves for or against the Peking regime. They have therefore remained relatively free in their handling of the China question, and their relations with the PRC have fluctuated from year to year with the vagaries of the political winds. The most important determinants of Japan's China policy have been, on the one hand, its military treaty with, and economic dependence on, the United States and, on the other, the demands of domestic interests for increased trade with China. The Japanese position is made unusually complex by widespread sympathy for new China and antipathy for the nuclear-armed United States: both sentiments derive from the Second World War, which left Japan divided socially just as it left Korea and Vietnam divided geographically. The weather-vane of Sino-Indonesian relations has been the status of the large community of overseas Chinese in Indonesia. The hostility of both countries to Western 'imperialism' has tended to draw them together, but more powerful factors—notably race and religion—keep them apart. A Malay and predominantly Moslem people, the Indonesians aspire to a wider hegemony in South-east Asia, and this makes them potential competitors of the Chinese Communists. Both can find historical precedents to bolster such ambitions: for instance, at different times each has exercised suzerainty over the Malay peninsula, an area in which, today, the Malay and Chinese populations are about equally balanced.

In 1949 about ten million overseas Chinese lived in South-east Asia, and some two million, or one-fifth, of them lived in Indonesia.

Overseas Chinese had come to South-east Asia around the turn of the century. Stable European rule—or, in the case of Thailand, a regime which aped European rule—drew them to the colonies just as it drew their countrymen to the treaty ports in China itself. Though they generally came as labourers, their frugality and ambition enabled many to enter the entrepreneurial class. The withdrawal of the Europeans following the Second World War left the Chinese in a dominant commercial position in Indonesia and several other South-east Asian countries. Their greater prosperity was a source of irritation to the local people. During the post-colonial era, ill treatment of the overseas Chinese has been limited primarily by the fact that their removal from the scene would mean economic chaos, and only secondarily by such pressure as Peking and Taipei could bring to bear on the South-east Asian governments.

Until 1953 the PRC tried to exploit the overseas Chinese for political purposes, but this policy did not bear fruit. It subsequently tried to merge pro-Peking activists among the overseas Chinese with the Communist parties of their respective countries of domicile. At the same time, Peking's attitude toward the overseas Chinese in general underwent a change. Whereas it had previously insisted that the overseas Chinese were Chinese citizens by blood (*jus sanguinis*), it now came to accept the idea that they were nationals of the country in which they were born (*jus soli*). Indonesia's Chinese population of about two million was one of the largest in South-east Asia, and its difficulties in the post-colonial era reflect those which nearly all overseas Chinese in South-east Asia have experienced. China and Indonesia had established diplomatic relations in 1950, and in 1954 they began negotiations on the problem of the overseas Chinese in Indonesia, many of whom claimed to be citizens of both China and Indonesia. A treaty dealing with the dual-nationality issue was signed in 1955, but ratifications were exchanged only in 1960. In any case, the treaty did not solve the problem, for it could not remove the hostility between the Chinese and the Indonesians. By the end of 1960 nearly 100,000 overseas Chinese had given up their residence in Indonesia and emigrated to the People's Republic of China. The situation of Indonesia's overseas Chinese deteriorated further following the downfall of President Sukarno in 1965.

Sukarno had tried to govern the country by balancing three rival claimants to power: native organizations based on religion; the army; and the Indonesian Communist Party (PKI), the largest Communist party outside the Communist bloc. Externally, he aligned Indonesia with the Soviet Union and the PRC. In his campaign to seize West Irian (western New Guinea), successsful in 1962, he enjoyed support from both countries. China's support was political; it also offered military advice which was reflected in the infiltration tactics employed by the Indonesian forces. Whereas the PRC did not provide arms, the Soviet Union established a massive programme of military aid for Indonesia which was a factor in the eventual emergence of the army as the dominant political force in the country. China also voiced support for Sukarno's policy of 'confrontation' with Malaysia which began in 1961 and became acute following the establishment of the new state (embracing, in addition to Singapore and Malaya, north Borneo territories bordering on Indonesian territory) in 1963. President Johnson's announcement in December 1963 that the US Seventh Fleet would extend its activities from Far Eastern to Indian and Indonesian waters provided a new bond between Peking and Djakarta. Sukarno had long supported the PRC's claim to Taiwan, frustrated by the presence of the Seventh Fleet in the Taiwan straits. A veritable Djakarta–Peking axis emerged in the next few years. Early in 1965 Sukarno took his country out of the United Nations and on 17 August, the tenth anniversary of Indonesian independence, he said that it was just a matter of time before his country embraced socialism (i.e. Communism). This entire edifice collapsed in the autumn of 1965, however, when the army seized control of Djakarta and initiated an anti-Communist bloodbath on a scale which the world had not seen since Chiang Kai-shek's coup in 1927.

China's relationship with her other island neighbour, Japan, was in large measure determined by the San Francisco peace treaty of 1951, denounced as invalid by the PRC. Neither Communist nor Nationalist China had been invited to the conference which drew up the treaty. That the treaty was intended to favour the Nationalists was indicated in the following year, however, when Japan signed a peace treaty with Taipei without making any corresponding gesture toward Peking, by then already engaged in the Korean War. While in San Francisco, the representatives from Tokyo and Washington agreed upon a security pact which would permit the US to maintain its forces in Japan after the occupation came to an end in April 1952. The Soviet Union established an embassy in Tokyo in 1956, but Japan's dependence on the US has been such as to preclude the establishment of diplomatic links with Peking.

The conservative governments which have controlled Japan since the end of the occupation have been regarded by the PRC as American puppets which do not reflect Japanese opinion. Consequently, Peking has sought to supplant the existing government, controlled by the Liberal Democratic Party, with one more to its liking. To this end it has given encouragement to the Japanese Socialist Party as well as the Japanese Communist Party, but this policy has had no serious effect. At the same time, however, Peking has favoured the expansion of Sino-Japanese trade, arranged through 'private' channels. Initially, the PRC's aim in promoting trade was mainly political. It hoped, by tempting Japanese manufacturers with the prospect of a vast China market, to bring sufficient pressure on the Liberal Democrats to force a change in Japan's overall foreign policy. In particular, the PRC wanted Japan to renounce its security treaty with the US, which had been negotiated in 1954 and, despite Peking's denunciations, renewed in 1960. The political content of Sino-Japanese trade was made apparent in May 1958, on the eve of a general election in Japan, when the Chinese Communists suspended all trade arrangements in an obvious attempt to embarrass Kishi, the incumbent prime minister. The pretext for the suspension of trade was the Japanese government's refusal to allow the Chinese trade mission in Japan to fly the PRC flag. Since the Sino-Soviet split, however, trade with Japan has acquired real economic importance for China. Peking relaxed its political demands so that trade might be resumed in 1960. It is certain that the significance of China's relations with Japan, industrially the world's third most powerful country, will grow. Japanese interest in China is shown by the fact that China receives more visitors from Japan each year than from any other country.

The national minorities: Tibet

Some 50 ethnic groups in China are distinguished from the majority population of 'Han' Chinese. The Han (named after the Han Dynasty, 206 BC–AD 222) people comprise about 95 per cent of the population but, in 1949, inhabited no more than 50 per cent of the area of the country. In general, the Han Chinese inhabited the best agricultural land, leaving the mountains, steppe, and other less desirable regions to the national minorities (many of whom are pastoralists). These national minority regions, part of the imperial realm inherited by the Chinese Communists, are situated on the frontiers of the PRC. Mongols in the north, Turkic peoples in the north-west, Tibetans in the west and south-west, and Tai peoples in the south are the principal groups. Following Soviet practice, the PRC established a separate administrative area for each national minority. It was realized that the evolution of the national minorities toward socialism might take slightly different paths, and proceed at different speeds, as compared with the Han majority. In principle, a wide degree of cultural autonomy, including preservation of their languages and religions, was granted the national minorities.

The establishment of autonomous areas for the national minorities fell mainly in the period of the mid-1950s, though it began as early as 1947 (with the Inner Mongolia Autonomous Region) and continued until 1965 (Tibet Autonomous Region). In general, administrative areas established for the national minorities parallel the regular administrative units: the autonomous regions, of which there are five, are equivalent to the province, and there are over ten times that number of nationality *hsien*, or counties. Another administrative unit, the *chou*, or prefecture (between the *hsien* and the province in size), is used in national minority regions but not among the Han Chinese.

The great care which the PRC has devoted to the implementation of its national minority policy reflects its concern lest the sudden imposition of central government control spark resistance among the non-Han peoples, who were only loosely administered under the empire and not really administered at all during the first half of the twentieth century. Moreover, the new regime envisaged a sizeable migration of Han persons—cadres, workers, farmers, technicians— to the frontier regions, which were short of skilled and industrious labour but extraordinarily rich in natural resources. The PRC's national minority policy represents a conscious attempt to minimize the friction which would inevitably arise between the national minorities and the Han Chinese. Han migrants to national minority areas have been pumped full of ideas of mutual respect and equality of treatment, and this indoctrination has not been without effect. On the other hand, conflict has occurred, the most serious instance being the Tibetan revolt of 1959.

Of all the principal non-Han peoples inhabiting China's frontier regions in 1949, the Tibetans were perhaps the most isolated and the most backward. In Tibet, thanks largely to the physical remoteness of the country, an essentially medieval social system had been perpetuated into the twentieth century. Tibetan Lamaism, a blend of Buddhism and the Tibetan animistic beliefs known as *bon*, was the state religion. The social ideal was for each family to send a son to a monastery and assume responsibility for his maintenance. Monks comprised one-sixth of the population. Ultimate authority in this theocratic state was wielded by the lamas, with the Dalai Lama as a sort of god-king. During the 1950s it became apparent that socialism could not be grafted onto Tibet's inherited social system. Tibetan resistance to change, especially among the lamaist hierarchy, and the CCP's determination to induce change, produced an explosive mixture which was ignited by the Dalai Lama's flight from Tibet in March 1959.

Chinese Communist troops had first entered Tibet in October 1950. After some clashes between the PLA and local Tibetan forces, an agreement was reached in May 1951 between Peking and Lhasa for the 'peaceful liberation' of Tibet. This was regarded at the time as a victory for the 'united front' policy of cooperating with religious and national leaders of the minorities, but it meant that the theocratic structure of the Tibetan state came through liberation unscathed. The Chinese, both military and civilian, who entered Tibet during the early post-liberation years lived apart from the Tibetans. Peking's control was exercised by General Chang Kuo-hua, commander of the Tibet military region, while matters affecting the Tibetan population were referred to the local Tibetan authorities. In 1956 a Preparatory Committee for the Tibet Autonomous Region was set up, with the Dalai Lama as chairman. In the same year two highways linking Tibet with China were completed.

The trouble began not in Tibet proper but in adjacent areas of Szechwan province inhabited by the Khamba, a people of Tibetan culture. 'Socialist transformation', for which Tibet itself was judged not yet ripe, was introduced among the Khamba in 1956. Since the Khamba are herders (unlike most Tibetans, who are agriculturists), 'socialist transformation' for them meant the pooling of their livestock in cooperatives. The Khamba resisted, and in the fighting which ensued bands of Khamba drifted eastward into Tibet proper, where they aroused the people against the Chinese. The Dalai Lama was then in New Delhi, as the guest of Prime Minister Nehru. Chou En-lai, who was also visiting India at the time, talked with him there and persuaded him to return. So anxious were the Chinese to smooth things over that they undertook to withdraw the bulk of their troops from Tibet and declared that basic social reforms would be indefinitely deferred. Nevertheless, fighting with the Khamba continued. The

Chinese, roadbound in a strange country, were constantly harassed by Khamba guerrillas.

The commune movement among the Khamba in Szechwan, introduced in late 1958, apparently had anti-Buddhist overtones. The lamas in Tibet no doubt satisfied themselves that it was but a matter of time before they experienced similar campaigns. They decided to seize the initiative. The revolt began during the new-year festival in March 1959. Khambas who had filtered into Lhasa and its environs played a major part in the struggle. They were joined by the local Tibetan army. Within two weeks, the Dalai Lama, who had fled Lhasa when the fighting erupted, reached the Indian frontier. In exile, he brought the struggle of the Tibetans to the attention of the world. The loss of Tibetan lives in the fighting is believed to have run to several tens of thousands. The International Commission of Jurists, in a report of 1960, referred to the PLA's suppression of the revolt as 'genocide', but the evidence presented was not convincing.

One of the steps reportedly taken by the Chinese Communist authorities in the aftermath of the revolt seems the reverse of genocidal: they forced many lamas to take wives. What is certain is that the lamaseries were virtually emptied. Only about one per cent of the lamas were permitted to remain; they were assigned to a few lamaseries designated as national monuments. The other 99 per cent were obliged to turn to productive labour. The lands belonging to the lamaseries were distributed to the peasants. In short, Tibet experienced its long-delayed 'democratic reform'.

The second-ranking religious personality in Tibet, the Panchen Lama, denounced the revolt. He was named Acting Chairman of the Preparatory Committee for the Tibet Autonomous Region. Despite the fact that the Panchen Lama had been educated entirely in China, however, he soon went the way of his predecessor. At the end of 1964 he was denounced for uttering public statements sympathetic to the Dalai Lama, who was still in exile. The Panchen Lama was replaced by a Tibetan aristocrat with stronger pro-Chinese inclinations. After 'elections' had been held in all of Tibet's 2,000 *hsiang*, a process which extended over a period of three years, the Tibet Autonomous Region was formally established on 1 September 1965, bringing to a conclusion the PRC's task of reorganizing the administrative structure of the country.

The CCP encountered unusually formidable obstacles in carrying out its national minority policy in Tibet. Tibet's pretensions to independent statehood, though not formally recognized by any third party, were a vexatious matter. The Khambas were an extremely troublesome people, and had always been so. In their way of life the Khambas were quite different from the people of Tibet proper, but the spiritual affinities between the two peoples were strong. The Khambas received external support. After they had established a base area in Nepal, if not before, they received military supplies by air-drop. The supplier was most likely Taiwan, which was also dropping material to anti-Communist forces on the China–Burma border. Tibet's semi-independent status and external ties were unmatched by any other major national minority area in China. Perhaps more important, the Tibetans had no prior experience of living together with Han Chinese, in contrast with most of China's non-Han peoples. In 1949 Han Chinese constituted one-half of the total population of all the national minority areas taken together, but in Tibet their number was nil. For these and other reasons, Tibet is an extreme case with respect to the application of the CCP's national minority policy. Though the CCP's achievements elsewhere have not been uniform, it is evident that the Chinese Communists have been successful in engaging the participation of most of the national minorities in the tasks of national construction, and many of them are well on the way to assimilation.

Border agreements

Between 1960 and 1963 the PRC concluded border treaties with Burma, Nepal, Mongolia, Pakistan, and Afghanistan, thus putting her relations with most of her immediate neighbours on a firm basis. The only non-Communist states contiguous to China with which the PRC has not concluded border agreements are India and Laos. In the case of India, the claims of the two sides are too far apart to admit of fruitful negotiation. The customary boundary between Laos and China has not been disputed; in any case, the Laotian government does not exercise any real control over its Communist-infested frontier areas adjacent to China and North Vietnam. The PRC's customary boundaries with North Korea and North Vietnam are also accepted, although in the case of the Sino-Korean border there is a mountain range which is claimed by both sides. China does not accept its existing frontiers with the Soviet Union, which were, according to a Peking statement of 1963, imposed by unequal treaties. The territories 'lost' to Tsarist Russia in the nineteenth century and now claimed by the Chinese involve half a million square miles of Siberia and Soviet Central Asia. China's frontiers with Bhutan and Sikkim are matters for negotiation with New Delhi, since these Himalayan states are Indian protectorates.

The PRC utilized the border settlements concluded during the early 1960s to obliquely criticize India and the Soviet Union, the two states with which she has outstanding frontier quarrels. The signing of the border treaty with the Mongolian People's Republic was hailed in Peking as proof that all problems between Communist countries could be solved 'in accordance with the principles of Marxism-Leninism and the principles guiding relations between fraternal countries laid down in the 1957 Moscow Declaration and the 1960 Moscow Statement'. Moscow, according to Peking, had trampled on these principles in its relations with the PRC. Similarly, Peking hailed the border settlements with Burma, Nepal, Pakistan, and Afghanistan as victories for the Five Principles of Peaceful Coexistence, which India, according to the Chinese, had persistently violated. The PRC described the boundary problems it had inherited as 'questions left over from history'. The particular historical period from which they dated is the second half of the nineteenth century, when foreign empires intruded upon a weak China. Peking was vexed by the refusal of New Delhi and Moscow to admit that their boundaries with China were the legacy of British and Tsarist aggression against China and that they should therefore be renegotiated.

Arrangements for overland trade and the establishment of consulates were in many cases agreed upon during negotiation of the border treaties. Such agreements reflected Peking's desire for improved communication with her immediate neighbours. Even Laos and Nepal are now linked to China by motor road, while Burma and Pakistan have air transport agreements with the PRC. China, for the first time in real control of her frontier regions, is in closer contact with her neighbours than ever before. In many cases the frontier is straddled by a single ethnic group: for instance, the Mongols live on both sides of the Gobi Desert, which separates the Mongolian People's Republic from the Inner Mongolia Autonomous Region; the former maintains a consulate at Huhehot, the capital of the latter. The Sino-Soviet frontier in Central Asia is also artificial with respect to ethnic divisions, for Kazakhs, Kirghiz, and other groups live on both sides of the boundary. This frontier has been tense for several years: each side suspects the other of trying to stir up tribal unrest.

Partly for this reason, work has long since ceased on the Sino-Soviet rail link through Sinkiang, which was to have been completed in 1962.

Burma has occupied a very special place in the foreign policy of the PRC. As a vassal state of the Ch'ing empire, Burma ranked behind only Korea and Vietnam in the intimacy of its relationship with China. Burma and India were the first non-Communist states to recognize the PRC; in 1954 it was with these two states that Chou En-lai first espoused the Five Principles of Peaceful Coexistence. Premier U Nu visited Peking many times; in 1961 he even took his family for a vacation in China's Yunnan province, which borders on Burma. Rangoon has cooperated with Peking in attempts to eliminate remnant Nationalist troops lodged in north Burma, going so far as to allow PLA units to enter north Burma for this purpose. However, General Ne Win, who ousted U Nu as head of the Burmese government in 1962, appears to be less well disposed toward the PRC than was his predecessor. During 1967, Sino-Burmese relations were hurt by anti-Chinese agitation in Rangoon.

The southern tip of China is less than 100 miles from the northern tip of Thailand, and the same hill peoples live in northern Thailand, southern China, and the intervening portions of Burma and Laos. These links are reinforced by history, Thailand being, like Burma, a former vassal of the Chinese empire. Thus, the fact that the two countries do not have a common frontier does not exclude the possibility of overland contacts. To date, there have been no official relations between Peking and Bangkok, where the South-east Asia Treaty Organization has its headquarters. Whereas the PRC has established diplomatic relations with all the states with which she has common frontiers, Thailand has remained a staunch friend of the United States and Taiwan. Perhaps she could afford to do so precisely because she does not border directly on China. Peking has repeatedly denounced the military regime in Bangkok for allowing the US to use Thailand as a base for aggression against Laos and North Vietnam, while Bangkok has just as frequently aired its suspicions that Communist China was promoting subversion in Thailand. In February 1965 the PRC removed all doubts in this connection by publicly announcing its support for an insurgency movement in Thailand which Peking referred to as the Thai Patriotic Front. Meanwhile, the US military build-up in Thailand has continued. Happily, the government in Bangkok has not been led by its security problems vis-à-vis the PRC to adopt repressive measures toward the more than two million overseas Chinese in Thailand. The Chinese community in Thailand is one of the three major overseas Chinese communities in South-east Asia, the other two being in Malaysia and Indonesia. Unlike the Malay and Indonesian Chinese, however, many Chinese have been quite successfully assimilated by the Thai community.

The nature of China's frontier areas has changed dramatically since 1949. Previously backward and bandit-infested, loosely or ill governed, they have now been politically stabilized and pushed forward on the road to modernization. Whereas they were traditionally a barrier to communication, these frontier regions now afford direct contact between China and her neighbours. No longer does China sit passively behind her frontiers, the object of the actions of others; rather, she reaches out across these frontiers to influence others. The conclusion of border agreements between China and most of her neighbours marks the end of an epoch.

CHAPTER EIGHT

A Maoist China

Economic re-adjustment and recovery

Following the Great Leap Forward (1958–60) and the withdrawal of Soviet technicians, the PRC entered a phase of fundamental re-adjustment in her domestic and foreign policies. The shift in economic policy was especially dramatic. Two five-year plans (1953–57 and 1958–62) had brought about very rapid expansion of the economy, but they had also produced serious imbalances. Having tried the Stalinist method of highly centralized, capital-intensive economic development during the period of the First Five-Year Plan, and having experimented with a decentralized and labour-intensive policy during the Great Leap Forward, the CCP now had to break new ground. As China's planners groped for solutions, traditional patterns of production and trade tended to re-emerge. The very concept of the five-year plan has apparently been abandoned. China's Third Five-Year Plan should have run from 1963 to 1967. Only in 1965, however, was any reference made to it. At that time it was said that the Third Five-Year Plan would begin in 1966, but no details were published.

The key elements in the CCP's effort to restore the economy were, first, recognition of agriculture as the most important sector of the economy and, second, use of material incentives throughout the economy. Western-trained economists had long argued that the development of the Chinese economy was highly dependent on agriculture. In China, agriculture employs most of the population, provides most of the raw materials for light industry, and accounts for most of the nation's exports. The attention of the CCP had been fixed on the agricultural front since 1959; it gave formal recognition to the primacy of agriculture at the tenth plenum of its Central Committee, which met in September 1962. By early 1963 the rural economy was back on its feet, but the grim three-year period of 1959–61 was not soon forgotten.

Grain production
(million metric tons)

1957	185
1960	150
1961	162
1962	174
1963	183
1964	200

The recovery proved costly to the regime in ideological terms, for in order to restore agricultural production it had to permit the restoration of private plots and free markets. At the same time, reliance was once again placed on the price mechanism in order to correct the dislocations which had resulted from bureaucratic management.

The devolution within the commune which had been authorized by the August 1959 eighth plenum robbed it of much of its original justification, but it did not disappear. The production brigade (corresponding to the natural village) or the even smaller production team became the unit of accounting, which meant that it was within that unit, rather than in the impersonal agglomeration of the commune, that profit and income were calculated. This change gave the peasant a much more direct stake in agricultural production. The commune movement and the Great Leap Forward had proved that the Chinese peasant simply would not put forth his maximum effort if there was no prospect of tangible rewards: the peasant could not be turned into a rural counterpart of the industrial proletariat, expected to perform an impersonal task each day in return for a subsistence allowance. Another important effect of the devolution within the commune was to halt, except for extraordinary projects, the mobilization of labour on a commune-wide basis. The separation of the peasant from his native village had been a kind of disincentive. Thus, the process of devolution within the commune would undoubtedly have led to some improvement in agricultural output even if there had not been a simultaneous restitution of material incentives.

Nevertheless, the commune remained, both as an administrative and as an economic unit. It continued to function as the lowest level of government administration. This role was reinforced by the correspondence which generally existed between the commune and the typical marketing areas of rural China. Such an area comprised a market town surrounded by perhaps 20 villages which depended on it. Given traditional means of transportation and the existing level of technology in agriculture, this was the optimum size for such marketing areas and it had become standardized through centuries of use. One weakness of the communes had been the attempt on the part of politically-minded cadres to force trading patterns to conform precisely to the administrative boundaries of the communes. Such precision was unnatural, and was soon corrected with the return to the price mechanism. For some purposes, some individuals in some villages would prefer to avail themselves of some market town other than the 'normal' one. What was true of individuals was also true of production teams, or the agents acting for them. Such subtleties often escaped the notice of the politically-oriented cadres who had taken charge of production during the Great Leap Forward. By 1962, however, the regime could appreciate the functional importance of the traditional marketing system with which the commune, perhaps unintentionally, had been integrated. Thus, the commune had real economic as well as administrative viability, though not precisely in the ways originally intended. After 1962 the commune became the unit for the modernization of the rural economy, a gradual process which will continue for many years.

One of the most striking indicators of the modernization of the rural economy is electrification. Small power plants, often owned by the commune, now make power available to most villages in China: in 1964 the consumption of electricity in the countryside was 23 times the 1957 level. During the same period the number of tractors increased five times. Nevertheless, the mechanization of Chinese agriculture remains a distant objective: for the present, the typical commune must content itself with modest improvements, such as the fitting of the traditional high-wheeled cart with iron tyres. While many of the local industries established during the Great Leap Forward proved inefficient and were subsequently scrapped, others proved their worth. The 'backyard furnaces' did show the peasants that it was possible to do things in the village which they had never dreamt of doing before. Today, many communes have their own machine shops and small-scale factories for meeting their own needs. This localized production has reduced the load on the nation's transportation network and led to many savings. 'Handicrafts', many of which now actually employ machinery, have regained much of the importance they lost to modern industry during the early years of the PRC. The following table shows the way the percentage of the national product accounted for by agriculture, modern industry, and handicrafts has fluctuated:

	1952	*1958*	*1962*
Agriculture	48	38	47
Modern industry	12	25	15
Handicrafts	7	5	6
Other	33	32	32

China's rural economy has, since 1962, reclaimed its old cellular pattern. Local agriculture supplies local industry, which in turn supplies the local market. This makes it possible for the commune to take advantage of idle labour during the slack season in agriculture and to ease the problem of under-employment in the countryside which had been characteristic of rural China for at least a century. These benefits could not have been realized if China had looked exclusively to large-scale production, either capitalist or Stalinist.

From the end of 1960 to the end of 1963 the PRC imported about 16 million metric tons of grain, chiefly from Canada and Australia. These imports were equivalent to only about three per cent of China's domestic food crop, but to at least 30 per cent of grain collected by the state. It was the failure of the countryside to produce a collectable surplus for urban consumption which necessitated these grain purchases abroad. On a reduced scale these purchases continued after agricultural production had been restored in 1963, suggesting that difficulties were still encountered in transferring grain surpluses from country to city. During the three-year period 1960–62, China sold over US$100 million in silver bullion in Europe to cover the deficit in her balance of trade caused by these grain purchases.

Although the extreme regimentation of commune labour did not outlive the Great Leap Forward, it was not without positive results. By 1960 it was claimed that 60 per cent of China's cultivated area had been irrigated. This was achieved by peasants working together to construct storage pools, ditches, and canals. Irrigation, flood control, and water conservancy are among the principal means available to the regime for raising agricultural output. They can be furthered by the application of machinery, some of it made in the communes' own workshops, and by the use of power, especially electric power, for pumping and other purposes. Thus, the modernization of the rural economy can directly serve the overriding need to raise agricultural output. Production per worker must be increased if China's food shortage is to be overcome and her investment requirements are to be met, for per capita food output largely determines the rate of saving throughout the economy, as well as the level of consumption. The supply of tractors and chemical fertilizers is still a long way from abundance, although both items are now five times as plentiful as they were in 1957. Nor does the reclamation of land or the migration of people provide an adequate alternative to increased productivity. These facts have become obvious to the regime and also, presumably, to the people living on the land. Thus, the commune experiment has revealed a powerful incentive system, though material incentives have also played a part. Agricultural output has been expanding steadily since 1962–63. Complete statistics are not available, but it appears that an annual grain crop of at least 200 million metric tons was harvested in 1964, 1965, and 1966. The 1967 harvest is said to be the best ever but, due to the enormous increase in China's population, the per capita supply of grain may be only a little better than it was in 1957. However, there is a much wider variety of food items available today than there was ten years ago.

The recovery of the industrial sector following the Great Leap Forward paralleled that of agriculture. By 1962–63 industrial production had been restored, and since 1964 it has been increasing at a rate of about 15 per cent per year compared with an overall rate of 10 per cent per year for the period 1949–65. As in agriculture, there has been an ideological price to pay for this expansion of industrial production. Not only have professional managers returned to their posts, displacing the CCP cadres who took charge during the Great Leap Forward, but a more attractive incentive system for the workers has come into effect. Production bonuses and piece-rate wages are among the inducements offered the ambitious worker.

The tenth plenum not only gave priority to agriculture over industry, it also put light industry ahead of heavy industry. Agriculture became the pace-setter; light industry was to support agriculture; heavy industry was to be the foundation for the whole economy, but the output of heavy industry was to be regulated by the needs of the other two sectors. Profits once more became the basis of decision-making in industry, as in agriculture. In the countryside the CCP cadres again turned an attentive ear to the opinions of the 'old peasants'; in industry, the technicians again had their say. The 1961 return to professionalism in industrial management was accompanied by the re-imposition of centralized control of planning, much of which had been delegated to local authorities. In fact, however, local authorities retained a good deal of power in economic decision-making. It was particularly difficult for Peking again to impose its will on the provinces. Local interests now began to compete with national interests.

The PRC's foreign grain purchases accentuated, but did not in themselves cause, the abrupt reorientation of China's overall trade from the Soviet Union to the 'free world'. Before 1949 China's principal trading partners were Western Europe, Japan, America, and South-east Asia; her trade with the Soviet Union and the countries of Eastern Europe was negligible. By 1952, however, trade with the Soviet bloc accounted for 75 per cent of the total trade of the PRC, and most of this was with the Soviet Union. The value of China's trade with the Soviet Union doubled between 1952 and 1959. It then declined precipitously. After 1957, the PRC maintained an export surplus in its trade with the Soviet Union in order to repay the credits previously received. In what must be one of the few instances in modern times of one state repaying in full the development credits extended by another country, by 1965 the PRC had completely paid off its debts to the Russians. Reflecting China's emergence as a regional power within the Communist bloc, the PRC's trade with North Korea, North Vietnam, and Mongolia did not decline after 1959, as did her trade with the Soviet Union and Eastern Europe (except Albania). The PRC's trade with the non-Communist world recovered gradually after 1952 as one country after another ceased to respect the special restrictions on trade with China which had been initiated by the UN during the Korean War. By 1963 the total value of China's exports to and imports from the non-Communist world surpassed that of her exchanges with the Soviet bloc, reaching US$1·5 billion, nearly three times the 1952 level. In 1963 food imports made up 50 per cent of all non-Communist exports to China, but capital goods were also important. In that year the PRC bought a complete industrial plant from Japan, the first time such an arrangement had been made with a non-Communist country. The purchase from Japan of this plant, for the manufacture of synthetic fibre, was followed by the purchase of an artificial fertilizer plant from the

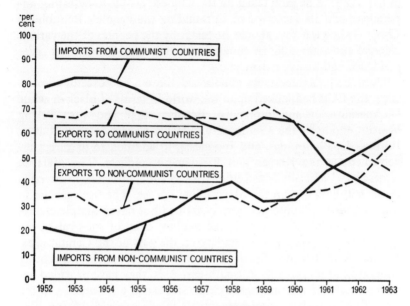

The changing direction of Communist China's trade

Netherlands. During 1963–64 China bought eight complete plants from Western Europe.

The underdeveloped world

The concept of a 'third world' lying between the Eastern and Western camps was an offspring of the cold war. The multitude of states in this zone, which stretches across Asia, Africa, and Latin America, were for the most part economically underdeveloped and politically unstable. With decolonization, which in less than 20 years doubled the number of UN members from 51 in 1945 to more than 100 in 1963, these states made up an area in which the more developed states sought to extend their influence. China had long felt drawn toward the third world. Li Ta-chao, the father-figure of Chinese Communism, had emphasized China's identity as a proletarian and a non-white nation. Such feelings were reinforced by Confucian universalism and shared by Chinese intellectuals of various political inclinations. Liu Shao-ch'i gave expression to this viewpoint when he said in late 1949: 'The path taken by the Chinese people in defeating imperialism and its lackeys and in founding the People's Republic of China is the path that should be taken by the peoples of the various colonial and semi-colonial countries in their fight for national independence and people's democracy.'

Until Stalin's successors announced the era of peaceful coexistence, the CCP had looked upon the world in terms of black or white —imperialist or anti-imperialist. Between 1948 and 1952 Peking heartily endorsed the Communist guerrilla movements in Malaya, Burma, the Philippines, and Indonesia, in addition to its direct involvement in the Korean and Vietnamese conflicts. The Malayan 'emergency' officially lasted from 1948 to 1960, but isolated guerrilla forces still hold out on the Malay–Thai border. The insurgencies in Burma and the Philippines were contained but never completely extinguished, while in Indonesia the military coup of 1965 raised the spectre of renewed guerrilla activity on the part of the Communists. To the extent that the PRC has been able to influence these and other underground movements in South-east Asia, they have provided her with a means of leverage against the established governments of the area. This remained true even after China's espousal of the Five Principles of Peaceful Coexistence in 1954.

Cambodia and Ceylon are examples of Asian countries which had slight contact with China before 1949 and generally good relations with China after 1949. Peking's relations with them have not been prejudiced by history or frontier problems, nor seriously troubled by problems of the overseas Chinese. Since both countries have followed a fairly consistent policy of neutrality with respect to the two power-blocs, the PRC's relations with them have provided good examples of China's general attitude toward the underdeveloped countries in Asia. Both countries have exchanged ambassadors with the PRC and accepted Chinese loans or grants for development projects. In relation to the third world, China is a comparatively developed country, able to supply a wide variety of industrial goods. The market afforded by China for Ceylonese rubber has been an important factor in the relations between the two countries, which have varied with domestic political changes and the international situation. The most decisive factor in Cambodia's relations with China is her fear and dislike of Vietnam and Thailand: she has been invaded by both countries in the past. Since they are allies of the US, it has seemed logical to Phnom Penh to seek security in an understanding with Peking. Suspicious of

Western intentions, Cambodia and Ceylon have done what they could to discourage a major US military presence in Asia and have thus helped China in her major foreign policy objective.

China's relations with the Middle East have hinged on Cairo and the cause of Arab nationalism. Peking did not reciprocate Israel's recognition, extended in 1950. Egyptian recognition in May 1956, followed soon afterwards by Syrian and Yemeni recognition, gave Peking a long-awaited opportunity to enter the Middle Eastern arena, but it proved ephemeral. What sympathy there is in the Middle East for the Soviet bloc has been to a large extent monopolized by the Russians, who have tolerated the suppression of Communist parties by the Arab governments. The Soviet Union has been able to establish a visible, if ineffectual, military role in the Middle East as the PRC has not. When the 1958 revolution in Iraq took Baghdad out of the Baghdad Pact, which had been organized by Dulles, both Peking and Moscow rushed to establish diplomatic relations with the Kassem government, which, however, was soon busy with the suppression of the Iraqi Communists. Perhaps the PRC's most durable tie with the Middle East is her need for Egyptian cotton.

Peking formally recognized the Algerian Provisional Government in September 1958: China was the first country of the Soviet bloc to do so. Thereafter, China supplied arms to the Algerian rebels and even offered to send volunteers. Sino-Algerian relations have remained friendly since the termination of the Franco-Algerian conflict in 1962. They were not affected by the 1964 establishment of diplomatic relations between the PRC and France, which was also, by that time, on good terms with Algiers. In North Africa the PRC also has relations with Morocco and Tunisia, although there is little cordiality in Sino-Tunisian relations.

A quarrel within the French Community also gave Peking its first opportunity of entering into relations with an African country south of the Sahara: in October 1959 it recognized the Guinean government, which was then at odds with Paris. In 1960 it established relations with Ghana, Mali, and the Somali Republic; in 1961 it recognized the secessionist regime in the eastern Congo which was fighting for its life against the UN-backed Congolese central government. In late 1963 and early 1964 Chinese Foreign Minister Chou En-lai made a goodwill tour of ten African countries. As of 1 January 1965, 11 African states, excluding North Africa and the UAR, had recognized the PRC, while 13 had diplomatic relations with Taiwan. The PRC has extended economic assistance to African governments which it considered revolutionary (that is, anti-imperialist). For example, Guinea obtained a US$25 million interest-free loan when President Sekou Touré visited Peking in the autumn of 1960.

During 1960 more officially-invited guests came to the PRC from Latin America than from any other non-Communist area. While Peking's diplomatic contacts with Latin America have been limited to Cuba, she is believed to have unofficial contacts with each of the 20 Latin American countries. Following the establishment of diplomatic relations in September, Ernesto Che Guevara, President of the Cuban National Bank, visited Peking in November 1960 and signed an economic cooperation agreement involving a Chinese grant of US$60 million. Something in excess of 100,000 overseas Chinese live in Latin America, one-third of them in Cuba. This is very small by comparison with overseas Chinese communities elsewhere. Apart from her evident desire to undermine US influence there, the PRC appears to have few if any vital interests in Latin America.

In South-east Asia, and in the Middle East as well, geographical proximity and a record of historical contacts provided a certain foundation for China's foreign policy. The China Buddhist Association and the China Islamic Association, both founded in 1954, were united-front organizations by which the CCP hoped to control Chinese Buddhists and Chinese Moslems and to influence their co-religionists in neighbouring states. The China Buddhist Association was headed by a Tibetan lama, while the Turkic governor of China's predominantly Moslem province of Sinkiang headed the China Islamic Association. Foreign policy toward black Africa and Latin America had to be developed in an unfamiliar environment. The PRC here had to rely on conventional means, such as aid programmes (the PRC extended more aid than it received after 1956) and radio broadcasts. In December 1964 Chou En-lai declared in a report to the National People's Congress that 'Asia, Africa, and Latin America have become the storm centres of world revolution at the present time'. Despite Chou's words, China's attempt to create and lead a bloc of underdeveloped, anti-imperialist states has so far been a lacklustre affair. During 1965 China campaigned vigorously for the convocation of a second Afro-Asian Conference, from which the Soviet Union would be excluded, but the fall of the Ben Bella government led to the suspension of preparations for the meeting, which was to have been held in Algiers.

India and Cuba

China's determination to have a road linking Tibet with Sinkiang, to the north, suggests that Khamba guerrilla activity had succeeded in making the eastern routes hazardous for Chinese convoys. There are also good economic reasons for the road, since Sinkiang has an exportable surplus of many food products which Tibet needs. The Sinkiang–Tibet route is known as the Aksai Chin Road because it passes through a thinly inhabited district of that name in Ladakh, which, though ethnically and culturally Tibetan, was attached to India by the British. The road was constructed in 1956–57, but was discovered by the Indian government only in 1958. In response to New Delhi's protest, Peking said that the area was really part of China. Sino-Indian relations took a turn for the worse following the Tibetan revolt in March 1959. Clashes between Indian and Chinese border guards occurred in the autumn. New Delhi adamantly refused to recognize the Chinese claim to the Aksai Chin area, while Peking declared that the entire Sino-Indian border was illegal and should be renegotiated in the spirit of the Five Principles of Peaceful Coexistence. The tacit support given the Indians by the Russians, who declared their 'neutrality' in the dispute, infuriated the Chinese. Peking did, however, enjoy the support of the Chinese Nationalists, whose frontier claims were even more extensive than the PRC's.

In mid-October 1962 India announced its intention to clear the Chinese Communists from the disputed territory by force, but the Chinese seized the initiative with an offensive of their own. The spectacular PRC attack, which began on 20 October, quickly overwhelmed Indian defensive positions and seized a large part of the North-east Frontier Agency, which lies far to the east of Ladakh. The main purpose of the Chinese 'invasion' was to establish a counter-claim to the Indian demand for the restitution of the Aksai Chin area. The PRC hoped it would be possible to induce the Indians to drop their Aksai Chin claim as a *quid pro quo* for Chinese withdrawal from the Northeast Frontier Agency, which Peking also claimed as a part of China. When New Delhi refused to negotiate on this basis, the PRC announced, on 21 November, a unilateral ceasefire and withdrew its forces from most of the territory seized.

Although India, with US, British, and Soviet assistance, had initiated a costly expansion of its military forces to repel the Chinese, there was little prospect of its being able to challenge the PLA in the Himalayas. China had shown its determination to hold the Aksai

Chin area. Any repetition of India's attempt to seize it could be expected to provoke Chinese counter-action elsewhere along the frontier, and the offensive of October–November 1962 had shown how
vulnerable India was. Sino-Indian relations have not improved since
the 1962 fighting and there has been no prospect of a comprehensive
border settlement.

When India began arming in order, as she said, to defend herself
against Chinese attack, Pakistan expressed apprehension that the
arms would ultimately be used against her. This is what happened in
the autumn of 1965, when hostilities were renewed between India
and Pakistan over the Kashmir issue. In this brief war India had the
sympathy of the Soviet Union as well as Britain and the United
States, while China threatened to intervene on the side of Pakistan.
This alignment dramatized the main effect of the Sino-Indian border
fighting of 1962, which had been to push India into a rigid anti-Chinese position in which it had the support of both Washington and
Moscow.

The Cuban missile crisis coincided with the border fighting between China and India. On 28 October 1962, Khrushchev capitulated
to the United States when he agreed to remove from Cuba the Soviet
missiles which were being installed there to defend Cuba against US
attack and, incidentally, to alter the world balance of power. The PRC
had played no part in this drama, but it castigated the Soviet withdrawal as a 'Munich'. Cuba, which had been invaded the previous
year by an army of exiles backed by the US, had cause for real concern for its security. Henceforth, the Cuban leader, Fidel Castro, and
radicals throughout Latin America would have to rely on their own
resources while perhaps looking to China for inspiration. The Soviet
Union followed up its Cuban fiasco by signing a partial test-ban
treaty with the US and the UK in the following year. The treaty
appeared to the Chinese as final confirmation, if any were needed, of
the Soviet determination to appease the United States at the expense
of China and the entire Soviet bloc. The test-ban treaty was as unpopular in Paris as it was in Peking and helped to draw the two countries together: they established diplomatic relations in January 1964.

A Fourth International?

Even before 1960 there had been a tendency for China to assert her
own, or an 'Asian', brand of Communism in her relations with other
Communist parties. Such an attitude was condoned by Lenin only a

few months after the May Fourth movement. At the Second All-Russian Congress of Communist Organizations of the Peoples of the East in November 1919, he told the delegates that in Asia they were

> confronted with a task which until now did not confront the Communists anywhere in the world: relying upon the general theory and practice of communism, you must adapt yourselves to peculiar conditions which do not exist in the European countries and be able to apply that theory and practice to conditions in which the bulk of the population are peasants, and in which the task is to wage a struggle not against capitalism, but against medieval survivals.

Marx himself, by introducing the notion of an 'Asian mode of production', had made it clear that his analysis of the forces of production applied mainly to Western society. It was thought, however, that divergent models of Communism, if they came into existence, would always be harmoniously related with one another. No one was more anxious to maintain Communist unity than Mao Tse-tung, who recognized long before 1949 that disunity meant weakness. Ideologically, nationalism was repugnant to him, even if he employed it effectively in seizing power and even if he was, in spite of himself, more Chinese than Communist. The appearance at Juichin and Yenan of Communists from Vietnam, Korea, and other lands did not indicate any schism between the CCP and the CPSU. The red base areas in China provided a good training ground for Asian Communists precisely because the Chinese Party was actually engineering a Communist revolution in an Asian country. There was no disloyalty in this. The fact that the hierarchies of the Vietnamese and Korean parties, both before and after seizing power, were divided between Soviet-trained and Chinese-trained members was not cause for comment or concern. Nor did the Russians begrudge their Chinese comrades a special role in the Communist movement in South-east Asia, especially after the failure of the insurrections in Burma, the Philippines, Malaya, and Indonesia, which had been triggered by Moscow in 1948.

The purpose of the meeting of 81 Communist parties which was convened in Moscow late in 1960 was to compose the differences between Moscow and Peking, but the result of the meeting was only to make clear to the leaders of the world Communist movement how far apart the Soviet and Chinese comrades were. The ensuing campaign of the CCP and CPSU to gain adherents to their respective ideological banners had the effect of splitting the world Communist movement. In general, the European parties took the side of Moscow, while the parties in Asia joined Peking. Some parties were split into pro-Soviet and pro-Chinese factions.

Virtually all Communists of Western Europe took the Moscow line, with Togliatti, the leader of the Italian party, serving as their spokesman. The Moscow line was also generally supported in Eastern Europe, where the Communist parties held power. For special reasons, Peking was able to gain the sympathy of the Albanian and Rumanian parties. In Asia, the CPSU had the strong and unequivocal support only of the Mongolian party, which it had installed in power 40 years earlier. The Communist parties in North Korea and North Vietnam divided into pro-Moscow and pro-Peking factions. Outside the bloc, the Indian and Japanese parties were also divided, but the pro-Moscow elements were strengthened by, respectively, the Sino-Indian border war of 1962 and China's detonation of an atomic bomb in 1964. The Indonesian party (PKI) was pro-Chinese, but the suppression of the party that began in late 1965 has made its future role in the Sino-Soviet split difficult to predict. It seems likely, however, that the PKI will become increasingly militant the more its numbers are reduced by government violence. A similar pattern may be expected in India, where the repression of pro-Chinese elements has led to increased revolutionary fervour among those who remain. In Ceylon followers of Peking quit the Communist Party in 1963 and formed themselves into a 'Marxist-Leninist' Party. As in Europe, the Communist parties in Latin America are predominantly in the Moscow camp. However, there are strong pro-Chinese tendencies in Brazil and Peru. The increasingly independent Cuban party is asserting its right to lead the Latin American Communist movement as a whole. The revolutionary fervour of the Cubans, voiced on such occasions as the 'Three Continents Conference' held in Havana in January 1966, is more enthusiastically applauded in Peking than in Moscow. The small and weak Communist parties in Africa and the Middle East have not played a significant role in the competition between the CCP and the CPSU for spheres of influence.

Between 1960, when the Sino-Soviet split became open, and 1963, when the Chinese began attacking the CPSU by name, it was the Yugoslav party which was featured as the arch villain in Peking propaganda. During the same period, Moscow directed criticism at Albania which was really intended for the PRC. Albania and Yugoslavia mark the extreme positions with respect to the issues raised in the Sino-Soviet dispute. By 1961 the Russians were following the Yugoslavs down the revisionist path, while the Chinese were cementing their relations with Albania, where a 'Stalinist' regime had been preserved in its purest form. Poland and Hungary, lying somewhere between Belgrade and Moscow in the ideological spectrum, have tried to use the Sino-Soviet split to increase their autonomy vis-à-vis the Soviet Union. The Communist Party of Rumania has sought to establish a special relationship with the CCP in order to protect itself against Soviet economic domination. The Chinese position has also found some support in the East German Communist Party.

Like China itself, North Korea and North Vietnam are territorially unsatisfied. Moscow's chosen policy of peaceful coexistence with the West offers little hope that their desires for national unity will ever be realized. This would appear to be the chief reason for Peking's success in winning their qualified support in the ideological struggle with Moscow. On the other hand, the Mongolian People's Republic, which is a territorially satisfied state and fearful of Chinese irredentism, has remained steadfastly loyal to Moscow. The PRC made a strenuous effort to establish close ties with all three states: between 1953 and 1961 the Chinese extended to them a total of US$900 million in aids and grants.

The assistance rendered by Peking in the Korean War and the Indochina War is another powerful factor in its favour in bidding for support in Pyongyang and Hanoi. That the PRC considers the defence of North Korea and North Vietnam vital to her own security cannot be doubted. In 1958 Peking had the good grace to bring home all Chinese forces which had remained in North Korea after the 1953 armistice. In 1956 the Chinese Communists made known their keen disappointment that the two-year deadline for the holding of all-Vietnam elections promised by the 1954 Geneva agreement had been allowed to pass. In doing so, they indirectly criticized the Soviet Union which, as co-chairman of the Geneva Conference, was theoretically responsible for implementation of the agreement. The renewal of widespread fighting in South Vietnam since 1961, with direct US involvement since 1965, has revived the question of the relative determination of the PRC and the Soviet Union to sustain their North Vietnamese ally.

The framework for a 'Chinese International' was established by the CCP Central Committee's eleventh plenum of August 1965, which called for a foreign policy which would oppose 'imperialism, all reactionary cliques of the world, and modern revisionism'—in plain words, the United States and its allies, all non-revolutionary governments in the third world, and the Soviet Union and its faithful satellites. Implicitly, the Chinese camp would include everything else. In an important article published just three weeks after the eleventh plenum, Marshal Lin Piao described the anti-imperialist, anti-revisionist forces as a kind of world countryside. Entitled 'Long Live the Victory of the People's War', the article commemorated the twentieth anniversary of the 'victory in the Chinese people's war of resistance against Japan'. Lin Piao suggested that Mao Tse-tung's theory of people's war, developed in the course of the struggle against Japan, could now be successfully employed against the United States which, on an international scale, was repeating the actions of Japan.

> Taking the entire globe, if North America and Western Europe can be called 'the cities of the world', then Asia, Africa, and Latin America constitute 'the rural areas of the world'. Since the Second World War, the proletarian revolutionary movement has for various reasons been temporarily held back in the North American and West European capitalist countries, while the people's revolutionary movement in Asia, Africa, and Latin America has been growing vigorously. In a sense, the contemporary world revolution also presents a picture of the encirclement of cities by the rural areas. In the final analysis, the whole cause of world revolution hinges on the revolutionary struggle of the Asian, African, and Latin American people who make up the overwhelming majority of the world's population. The socialist countries should regard it as their internationalist duty to support the people's revolutionary struggle in Asia, Africa, and Latin America.

Whereas the Chinese people were giving this struggle maximum support, Lin Piao said, it was being sabotaged by the Khrushchev revisionists in collusion with the US imperialists.

The Communist International was established in 1919 by a fledgling Bolshevik state surrounded by hostile forces which threatened to devour it. The recruitment of other nations into the Communist cause would not only serve Marxist-Leninist ideals, but would also help the Russians break out of their isolation. In recent years the Chinese Communists, in the same way, have felt themselves surrounded. Since its birth the PRC has been confronted by US power on its Pacific littoral. The danger from the US was at first offset by Peking's alliance with Moscow, but the Soviet Union is now considered more of an enemy than an ally and the 2,000-mile-long Sino-Soviet frontier has become another danger zone. China's encirclement is virtually completed by hostile India and Japan. At a press conference on 29 September 1965 Foreign Minister Chen Yi lumped these powers together, adding Britain:

> If the US imperialists are determined to launch a war of aggression against us, they are welcome to come sooner, to come as early as tomorrow. Let the Indian reactionaries, the British imperialists and the Japanese militarists come along with them! Let the modern revisionists [i.e. the leaders of the Soviet Union] act in coordination with them from the north! We will still win in the end. . . .

Thus, Lin Piao's thesis of encircling the cities of the world by the world countryside is really a policy of counter-encirclement.

China's nuclear weapons provide her anti-imperialist, anti-revisionist bloc with a measure of respectability, if not real security. China's first atomic bomb was detonated in October 1964; on 17 June 1967, after four additional atomic explosions, she set off her first hydrogen bomb. The H-bomb was carried aloft by a missile and detonated at a height of 20 miles. Nevertheless, China is not believed to possess, as yet, an intercontinental ballistic missile. China's nuclear programme received initial assistance from the Soviet Union, which built one or more experimental atomic reactors in China in 1956–57 and provided training in the Soviet Union for Chinese technicians engaged in this programme. Chinese nuclear scientists had earlier received training in France and the United States. After 1958 the Russians evidently came to the conclusion that it was not in their national interest to continue this assistance, and since that time the Chinese have been working on their own.

The Cultural Revolution

The movement which burst forth in China in the summer of 1966 under the title of the Great Proletarian Cultural Revolution was actually an attack on the Communist Party by its leader, Mao Tsetung. Mao had found himself increasingly at odds with the Central Committee ever since the Great Leap Forward, which was interpreted by many of his colleagues as a disaster brought on by specifically

Maoist policies. At the end of 1958 Mao relinquished his position as head of the government, and was succeeded by Liu Shao-ch'i. Although Mao retained formal leadership of the Party, his authority had been undermined. Mao did not like the policies introduced between 1959 and 1962: they were demonstrably effective in getting the national economy back on its feet and in easing tensions in China's external relations, but they had the effect of hobbling the revolution, and it was the revolution which was of prime interest to Mao. At the Central Committee's tenth plenum, held in 1962, Mao succeeded in winning approval for a 'socialist education' campaign designed to combat the re-emergence of class divisions in Chinese society; the abolition of military ranks in May 1965 was another Maoist victory. However, the 'Khrushchev revisionism' which Mao believed was beginning to infect Chinese functionaries could not be easily contained, and in September 1965 Mao was defeated in the Central Committee when he insisted that 'reactionary ideology' be more rigorously criticized.

Mao had the support of Defence Minister Lin Piao, who encouraged the movement to 'study Mao Tse-tung's thought'. The little red book of Mao's sayings, which was to be such a prominent feature of the cultural revolution, was distributed to the army in 1964. In April 1966 the *Liberation Army Daily* issued a call for a 'cultural revolution' to eliminate 'bourgeois ideology in the academic, educational, and journalistic fields; in art, literature, and all other fields of culture'. The campaign was initially directed against ideological deviations in the cultural field because it was there that the opposition to Mao had exposed itself most noticeably. In particular, a play by Wu Han entitled *Hai Jui Dismissed from Office* made use of an historical parable to defend P'eng Teh-huai, the Minister of Defence who had been fired by Mao in 1959. Wu Han happened to be the deputy mayor of Peking. Thus, it was the propaganda department of the CCP and the Peking CCP committee that first came under fire in the cultural revolution. Mayor Peng Chen and Minister of Culture Lu Ting-yi were among the best known of many persons removed from office. But it was apparent that Mao's opponents were deeply entrenched in the Party and government hierarchy throughout the country: in order to expose them, he unleashed the Red Guards.

Peking University students had been encouraged to demonstrate against their ousted president, Lu Ping, in June. Student agitation steadily increased thereafter. Red Guards participated in an enormous rally in Peking on 18 August 1966, during which Mao Tse-tung himself donned a Red Guard armband. Chiang Ch'ing, Mao's wife, and Ch'en Po-ta, his former secretary, became the mentors of the Red Guard movement. During the next three months Mao is said to have reviewed 11,000,000 Red Guards who poured into Peking from all over the country to participate in the great demonstrations being held there. Those who could not get onto the clogged railways made 'little Long Marches' to the capital. With all schools closed, revolutionary activity became the full-time occupation of China's students, a large proportion of whom were formally enrolled as Red Guards. Like the cultural revolution itself, the Red Guard movement opposed 'feudalism, capitalism, and revisionism'. The ire of the Red Guards was initially directed against the 'four olds'—old ideas, old culture, old customs, and old habits—which, it was held, still affected Chinese society. They destroyed cultural objects in private homes and public places. This phase of the movement was also xenophobic, persons with Western-style clothing or haircuts frequently being molested. Such was the revolutionary enthusiasm of the Red Guards that at street crossings they tried to make motor vehicles proceed on the red light and stop on the green. More serious was the humiliation of local officials. Many 'revisionists' and 'reactionaries' were beaten; some even died. Others succeeded in rallying the support of the local people, who engaged the Red Guards in pitched battles. Several days of street fighting in Nanking during January 1967 left 54 dead and 900 wounded. The Red Guard movement spread into the factories, where workers were encouraged to 'voluntarily' reduce their wages in order to check the growing influence of 'capitalism'. Clashes between Red Guards and workers occurred in many parts of China. In sum, the Red Guard movement was directed against China's new privileged classes.

In November the head of the government, Liu Shao-ch'i, was denounced as the 'Chinese Khrushchev' and as the 'top person in authority taking the capitalist road'. Not only did Mao believe that Liu sympathized with Khrushchev revisionism; he also thought that Liu would betray him just as Khrushchev had betrayed Stalin. The aging Mao Tse-tung did not want to pass on authority to a man who could be counted upon to denounce Maoism. Liu had particularly strong support from organized labour, with which he had long been identified. This circumstance partially explains why the cultural revolution was so critical of the industrial workers. Following the

Central Committee's eleventh plenum, held in August 1966, Liu had been dropped from the second to the seventh position in the hierarchy, while his place as appointed successor to Mao was taken by Lin Piao. Premier Chou En-lai remained in third place.

Mao was concerned about the outlook of the next generation of Chinese as well as with that of the individual who would succeed him, and part of the rationale of the cultural revolution was that it would give China's youth revolutionary experience. At the same time, it provided an opportunity to check the growing dominance of the universities by students of other than proletarian backgrounds. The great driving force behind the Red Guards was provided by middle-school students from peasant families who knew that, as things stood, they would not succeed in the competitive examinations for places in the universities, and failure in the examinations meant a career in the countryside. The admission of more such students to China's institutions of higher learning was an objective of the cultural revolution: the use of exclusively intellectual criteria for student admission had become reactionary by the time schools reopened in the autumn of 1967.

The cultural revolution was accompanied by an intensification of the cult of Mao Tse-tung—'the greatest genius of our time', according to the Peking *People's Daily* of 15 June 1966. Maoism, which had emerged during the Yenan period, developed strongly during the Great Leap Forward. When China veered away from the Soviet line of development, it had to turn to Maoism. There was no other alternative. If Maoism were then rejected, China would have to take up once again the latest intellectual vogue in Moscow which happened to be 'revisionism'. The People's Republic of China had been established as a part of the world socialist camp. The leaders of the PRC, Mao included, had claimed political legitimacy from Marxism-Leninism-Stalinism. The Sino-Soviet split seriously threatened this legitimacy, or right to govern. Maoism, which firmly rejected Soviet leadership, took its place. As Lin Piao said in his foreword to *Quotations from Chairman Mao*:

> Comrade Mao Tse-tung is the greatest Marxist-Leninist of our era. He has inherited, defended, and developed Marxism-Leninism with genius, creativity and comprehensively and has brought it to a higher and completely new stage. . . . Mao Tse-tung's thought is the guiding principle for all the work of the Party, the army and the country.

In other words, Mao is Lenin's successor as thinker and revolutionary. Production of Mao Tse-tung's *Works* became so feverish as to create a nation-wide paper shortage, while his stories and maxims were endlessly repeated by the nation's radio stations.

The cultural revolution undermined the authority of the CCP as the governing elite. During 1967 'revolutionary committees' began to be substituted for CCP committees in various provinces and municipalities. They were to include representatives of, firstly, the Red Guards and revolutionary workers; secondly, the army; and, thirdly, the existing Party and government organizations. Generally, the army was the key factor in the establishment of revolutionary committees. The PLA had played an important role in the cultural revolution, often intervening on behalf of Red Guards. In February 1967 it was ordered to check Red Guard excesses. However, the PLA did not itself attempt to seize authority from the Party or to determine the outcome of the cultural revolution. In a few places, such as turbulent Canton, the army for a time took over administration, but this was always of a temporary, emergency nature. In general, army units remained subservient to the local Party men, who might be either pro- or anti-Maoist. In places where they were staunch Maoists, revolutionary committees were established without much difficulty. Authorities in the outlying regions of Sinkiang and Tibet were notably noncommittal, with the result that revolutionary committees could not be established there. Strong anti-Maoist sentiments within the Party also found PLA support in other provinces throughout the country: in Wuhan, the struggle between Maoist and anti-Maoist forces turned into open warfare. In general, it was the poorer provinces which rallied to the Maoist standard, for they are dependent on the state for food shipments from the grain-surplus provinces. Conversely, the richer provinces had more incentive to resist the new Maoist order. As of August 1967 revolutionary committees had been set up in Heilungkiang, Tsinghai, Kweichow, Shansi, and Shantung, as well as in Shanghai and Peking. These two cities, which are dependent on imported grain, are in a weak political situation similar to that of the grain-deficit provinces.

The effects of the Great Proletarian Cultural Revolution have been felt beyond China's frontiers. Chinese diplomats have been criticized for their bourgeois tastes, and many have been recalled, leaving embassies almost empty. Partly in retaliation for desecration of Buddhist monuments in Tibet by Red Guards, Chinese officials in

New Delhi were beaten by Indian mobs. Pakistan, however, has remained on good terms with Peking despite anti-Moslem actions by Red Guards in China. The overseas Chinese have not been enthusiastic about the cultural revolution, but Maoist demonstrations by overseas Chinese have occurred. Tension between Chinese and Burmese communities was stirred up by a nascent Red Guard movement among Chinese youth in Rangoon. The Portuguese authorities in Macao were humbled by Maoist agitation, but in Hong Kong the British authorities succeeded in retaining control of the situation. Sympathy for China among Japanese has declined as a result of the cultural revolution, perhaps because it reminds them of their prewar experience with totalitarianism. The apparent militancy of the cultural revolution and its virulent anti-Soviet stance has tended to drive the Russians and the Americans together despite the war in Vietnam. The deterioration in Sino-Mongol relations, visible for some time, has been furthered by the cultural revolution, but Peking remains a powerful influence in North Korea and North Vietnam. Although economic relations with Western countries have been maintained, the cultural revolution has hurt China's image in Europe. In general, it appears that China now wishes to be friendly only with countries which, like Albania, are strongly opposed both to 'imperialism' and to 'revisionism', and with peoples who are actively engaged in revolutionary struggles, notably the South Vietnamese. Evidently, China would today like to remake the world in the Maoist image.

Index